The Good Enough Spouse

The Good Enough Spouse

Resolve or Dissolve Conflicted Marriages

By Dr. William E. Ward

New Horizon Press
Far Hills, New Jersey

New Horizon Press
P.O. Box 669
Far Hills, NJ 07931

Ward, Dr. William E.
The Good Enough Spouse: Resolve or Dissolve Conflicted Marriages

Cover design: Robert Aulicino
Interior design: Susan Sanderson

Library of Congress Control Number: 2011922559

ISBN 13: 978-0-88282-364-5
New Horizon Press

Manufactured in the U.S.A.

15   14   13   12   11   1   2   3   4   5

Dedication

To my children, whom I cherish:
Billy, Sean, Jacque and Brooke

Author's Note

This book is based on the author's research, personal experiences and clients' real life experiences. In order to protect privacy, names have been changed and identifying characteristics have been altered except for contributing experts. The basic dynamics of individuals' behavior and marital experiences have not been distorted. The illustrations are examples of the common areas that couples struggle and deal with on a regular basis.

For purposes of simplifying usage, the pronouns he/she and him/her are sometimes used interchangeably. The information contained herein is not meant to be a substitute for professional evaluation and therapy with mental health professionals.

Contents

Preface

Is Your Marriage in Trouble?

Most couples walk into divorce court without a clue about why their marriages are about to end. Some spouses are even heard to say, "You know, this didn't have to happen. We could have worked it out." Others remain angry, but they are reacting more to the emotional and mental consequences of divorce, still unaware of what led to such results. Couples, sometimes even marriage counselors, rarely discuss or have the ability to delve into the real reasons for the failure of so many marriages. Some explanation is often given for the divorce occurring but very few partners spend the time to get to the core of a marriage's demise.

The announcement of a pending divorce is especially surprising in long-term marriages. It is presumed couples married for twenty-five or thirty years or more have successfully passed through the rough stages and therefore their unions will last a lifetime. Yet, such is not the case in the last few decades. The divorce experience is affecting long-term marriages in greater numbers than ever before. The United States Census Bureau estimates that of the 50 percent of marriages ending in divorce,[1] 25 percent of new divorces ended unions of twenty years or more in 2008.[2] The end of long-term marriages is increasing in frequency due to longer life spans and new social acceptance of divorce.[3] It may come as a surprise that a friend, a relative or a celebrity is divorcing after many years, but outsiders do not know what is going on in another person's marriage. Two people deciding to divorce were most likely ignoring or simply putting up with the slow erosion of their relationship.

Whether it is a divorce in the early stages or after years of marriage, I believe the underlying problem remains the same. Most couples do not know how to identify their real issues, nor do they have the knowledge to resolve these issues before they become a major infection. Couples go through endless and repetitive conflicts without ever getting to the heart of why they occur in the first place. Once each partner learns to examine the relationship in greater depth, the repetitive nature of these conflicts is especially recognizable in long-term marriages. There is always a consistent pattern and an underlying theme in partners' interactions with each other. Unfortunately, this type of exploration is done more times after divorce, not before.

Even before marriage, these same couples may have ignored or at least passed over clashes and conflicts while dating. In doing so, they carried their psychological issues into their marriages. If they had addressed these issues before marrying, they might have had the chance to either correct the conflicts or discover the relationship was not a good match in the first place. In order to avoid the ongoing ignorance regarding marital relationships, the first and primary reality to be learned from this book is that there are concrete reasons for the success or demise of marriages. This is the purpose of this book: to take the mystery out of marriage.

If you have chosen this book, you most likely fall into one of four categories. First, you might be experiencing marital conflicts (everyone does) and you are looking for a new perspective to help you improve your marriage, fix some problems and create solutions you never thought of previously. You may be searching for a way to reverse the direction your marriage is going and to bring back to life the hope and dreams you had on your wedding day. Too many couples make the mistake of ignoring or passing over individual differences that lead to repetitive tension. One or both partners take on the silent response of resignation, convinced there is no other option. It is the same as ignoring a cavity in a tooth: an abscess occurs. It may take years, as seen in late-term divorces, but sooner or later the marriage begins to erode and the distance between the two partners grows.

Marital conflicts do not automatically mean the relationship is a poor one. In many cases, the solving of problems may be an opportunity to grow. Author Thomas Moore presents this perspective when he explains that problems "do not necessarily mean that there is something inherently wrong with the relationship; on the contrary, relationship problems may be a challenging initiation into intimacy."[4] Moore's comments are both insightful and encouraging. Specific problems may indicate something is off-kilter. By addressing the issues correctly, you have a chance to resolve the problems in order to allow for greater intimacy and growth.

Second, you might be part of the group in which the marriage has already dissolved. Perhaps you are still experiencing the emotional repercussions of the divorce. Or you might be looking for deeper insight about why the relationship failed. You realize it is a mistake to think the fault lies with only one person. In order not to go down the same path again, you want to be assured you know exactly what you are doing the next time. You realize that without this understanding, the odds are high you will repeat your errors. Even when a new partner seems totally different from your former spouse, it is you who is not. Without proper insight, you are likely to remarry for the same reasons you did the first time and make the same mistakes.

Third, you may be part of a relatively new marital phenomenon: the ending of a long-term marriage. More couples than ever before are calling it quits after twenty-five or thirty years of marriage. The initial reasons are multi-dimensional. The kids have grown up and left the house, freeing a partner of guilt for leaving dependent children. The marital conflicts have intensified or perhaps an affair was discovered. Conversations have become superficial and partners have lost respect for each other. As one husband stated, "I thought I could make her happy. But the cost was the loss of my true self." Or it may be because people are living longer and one or both partners do not want to carry on much longer in a relationship that is and has been for a long time causing them great unhappiness.

All the reasons for marital conflict and failure have veracity. But beneath each of these simple realities there is a more primary and complex truth. Long-term marriages do not end suddenly, no matter what the reasons given. It is similar to the fact that many of our physical cells have the potential to turn cancerous. Divorce is the consequence of two people living in an unhealthy manner. In many situations, it takes years for it to turn incurable.

Fourth, you may be single and seeking a love relationship. Of the four groups, this is the one that can best be called preventive. Many married couples, in hindsight, wish they had more awareness before they made the decision to marry. For those moving toward marital commitment, this book will help in choosing to be a partner for healthy reasons and avoiding the process of redundant mistakes. It will show you how to be a partner and build a partnership that will bring satisfaction and fulfillment.

Part One

Personal History and Marital Future

The success or failure of a marriage is not a mystery. There are concrete reasons why some partners continue to experience love, share respect and show ongoing compassion for each other. There are underlying reasons that explain how they are able to cooperate with each other in solving their day-to-day issues. In contrast, there are definitive reasons why marriages become disjointed and eventually fall apart, even though they began with the greatest of intentions. This is true not only for marriages that last for five or ten years, but also for the couples who shock their families and friends with divorce announcements after twenty or thirty years of marriage. In both cases, the reasons did not just suddenly appear. They were fermenting for the entire lives of the marriages.

Failed marriages and those in constant states of tension all share one thing in common: Day-to-day interactions are taken for granted and treated superficially. This is especially true when there are disagreements or conflicts. Rather than evaluating interactions and their outcomes and searching for ways to improve the relationship, couples bypass difficult times as if they will simply go away. Throughout their years of marriage, they allow situations, both positive and negative, to take place with very little thought or reflection as to why they occurred. It is as if these couples perceive marriage as having a life separate from themselves and not in their control. The couples treat their marital relationships as if they have wills of their own and some outside force will carry the couples through the lives of their marriages one way or another. The reason why marriages fail is not a mystery: They are allowed to fail.

Successful marriages occur when two people are both willing to work at understanding in greater depth who they are and why they do the things they do. Rather than allowing tension and arguments to simply take place time and time again, partners search for a deeper understanding of why conflicts occur in the first place. Successful marriages involve two people who are willing and have the courage to actively explore ways to do things better. Marriages do not succeed due to some outside force. The force and energy lies within each partner and the partners together.

Tom and Jennifer's Story

Tom and Jennifer were married for thirty-seven years. Tom had a financially successful medical practice and they both decided Jennifer should stay at home to take care of their three children. During the first five to ten years of marriage, everything seemed, at least on the surface, to be flowing well. Tom was busy finishing up school and beginning a private practice. Jennifer was actively engaged in taking care of the children, all born two years apart.

From the beginning, however, both were ignoring their financial responsibilities. Even though Tom was earning more than enough for the average couple, Jennifer always seemed to view money as if it were everlasting. Numerous vacations were taken at the best and most expensive hotels. They moved several times to bigger and more expensive houses and they bought furniture in the most elite stores.

Tom knew early on in the marriage that he was drowning in bills. He went to work daily knowing he had to make enough just to meet the daily and weekly financial requirements. But he also had the need to please his wife and provide for his children. He lacked the courage to say no to any of them. He remembered but chose to ignore his mother-in-law's warning prior to the marriage. She had said to him, mixing humor with seriousness, "I am going to watch how you deal with the golden spoon in her mouth."

No matter how many trips they took, how many houses they bought or the daily activities that required a great deal of money, Tom's attempts to please his wife were always short-lived. Once the children were adults and left home and the primary expenses were behind them, Tom decided he could no longer deal with the choking pressure of money. On dozens of occasions he pleaded with Jennifer to work with him on a plan to pay off their tremendous debt. She always agreed at first, but not five minutes later she always said something like, "When do you think we can plan a trip to Europe?"

Tom was growing older. Other issues began to arise where Tom found it impossible to please Jennifer. She always wanted more and tensions mounted as her demands grew. Tom was perplexed and often depressed in his failing attempts to please her. He listened to Jennifer's constant complaints of being unhappy. Though she had spent years threatening him with divorce, he was still surprised when the local sheriff handed him the notification of Jennifer's filing for divorce. To all who knew them, they were a fun-loving and happy couple. In reality, they were drowning in a pool of stress and misery.

Jennifer and Tom are not unusual. Even though the issues and demands might be different for every couple, ignoring destructive issues is more often the case than not. The common denominator for failed marriages is couples who hop into the marital car on their wedding days and allow it to take them for a ride. It is passivity at its worst.

Wishing and hoping for change take the place of work and insightful participation. It is as if each partner is saying, "If we get through it, lucky us. If it crashes, so be it." Failed marriages occur, because two people live within their marriage as if neither has any control in the direction it takes. Or, more typically, each blames the other partner if the direction takes a turn for the worse. Even though Jennifer was impossible to please, Tom was equally at fault for his lack of courage to say no.

With the increasing number of divorces, we have become accustomed, even immune, to the overabundance of marital failures. To the couples who remain married, many resort to the simplified attitude, "Well, some marriages last; others just don't." This passive attitude has obvious consequences, especially seen in the termination of long-term marriages. There is a price for ignoring the cavity or for just going along for the ride. There is no doubt that when a marriage fails it is both partners who are responsible for not taking control of the relationship with wisdom, insight and hard work.

Our marriages succeed for a reason and they fail for a reason. There is never a guarantee, but we do have more control over the outcomes of our relationships than we may think. However, it takes mutual cooperation for it to work. This is something Jennifer and Tom lacked. At the very least, they lost respect for each other. The key to a successful relationship is to understand, in depth, the role we personally play—be it healthy or unhealthy—in the relationship and why we play it. Beneath each and every marital interaction we participate in with our spouses, there are underlying reasons and purposes. The same holds true for our partners. The challenge is to get beyond superficial reactions and to search for insight.

Often I ask couples in therapy to view a particular conflict as a play. After both have explained to me a particular incident they recently experienced with each other that turned unpleasant, I ask them to pretend they are sitting in a theater viewing the incident on stage. I also have them pretend they are watching another couple go through the exact same interaction. This allows them to have some objectivity, rather than being so personally involved with fragile egos on the line.

As the three of us "watch" the play, the couple has the opportunity to observe each character, but this time from a deeper perspective. I ask them to look beneath the behavior for what each character may be thinking and feeling as each interaction takes place. Both husband and wife are asked to concentrate on the people playing their respective roles. They are asked to evaluate the performance as if they are trying to analyze another couple. I emphasize certain questions during our discussion, such as, "What do you think each person is feeling during the interaction?" "Are the partners being honest or is one or both reacting more to feelings of vulnerability?" "Does it feel like the partners are being defensive?" "Are they listening and trying to solve the problem or is one or both trying to win?"

As each partner goes through this exercise, it is amazing how differently he or she views the entire incident. Both partners are able to evaluate more objectively what each person might be experiencing, both emotionally and cognitively. They are able to observe inappropriate reactions and mistakes in behavior. As they discuss the "play" they are also able to come up with more creative responses that might change the total outcome. This is what working hard at a relationship involves.

In the case of Tom and Jennifer, each was asked several questions after viewing one of their "plays."

Questions to Tom:
- "Tom, why do you feel the need to always please Jennifer?"
- "Why do you think money will solve her needs?"
- "Have you tried to figure out what her real needs are?"
- "What do you do with your frustration and anger when you feel like it is endless?"
- "Tom, have you noticed distance growing between the two of you?"

Questions to Jennifer:
- "Why do you ignore Tom's worry and concern over money? Are you thinking of his needs?"
- "Do you see marriage as working as a team?"
- "You continuously demean Tom for not making enough money and say he could earn more if he worked longer hours. Do you worry about his well-being?"
- "Jennifer, have you noticed distance growing between the two of you?"

Most couples never take the time to consider their conflicts in this manner. With each troubling incident, they only react. This process is not only repetitive but also destructive. Over time, the marriage is drained of its vitality. Today, promise yourself to stop the vicious cycle. Promise yourself to stop protecting your ego and become more honest. Promise yourself that you will stop reacting and begin to learn.

Most psychologists agree there are underlying reasons for both productive behaviors and destructive behaviors. Knowing we have the potential for both forms of behavior and realizing we actually can do something about them is the main formula for achieving good relationships. Working at a marriage is hard work. It is much more difficult than just letting things happen, but this labor is the only way to achieve a successful marriage. The process may be onerous, but in the end it is so much more successful.

Let's take the mystery out of successful or failed marriages. It is more beneficial to consider marriage as one would consider attempting to solve a puzzle. An intimate relationship has many pieces which must be fitted together. To do this, one must learn how to put the pieces together, seeing where each piece fits and knowing that each piece is part of the bigger picture. The marital puzzle demands full cooperation on the part of both partners to be successfully completed.

A marriage cannot function without full participation and cooperation by each partner. Marriage is a challenge. The challenge involves working together toward trying to realize how each incident, no matter how large or small, affects us personally and affects our partners as well. The challenge involves—it mandates—that partners work together at creating healthy responses to each contentious issue. Without trying to understand the hidden dynamics underlying each and every marital interaction, marriage can zoom out of control like a car without a driver. It becomes an accident waiting to happen. Thomas Moore clearly made this point when he said, "One reason we may have so much trouble with relationships today may be out of neglect of its study. We expect to find intimacy naturally, without education or initiation into intimacy."[1]

Why people think marriage does not require work and study might be more of the mystery. Yet, people often fail to see the necessity for work in other areas of life also. Friendship takes work and understanding. Raising children takes work and understanding. Personal growth and development take work and understanding. Not to recognize and accept this necessity leads to failure in all areas of life.

In fact, work and study about marriage is more than a necessity: it is an obligation—one that many people avoid out of ignorance. Most people were never taught how to look into their lives in a deeper fashion. Others might dodge this task out of laziness, finding it easier to accept life in its simplest form. Even worse, some partners might sidestep looking deeper into their marriages out of fear of what they might discover and be forced to face. Whether it is ignorance, laziness or avoidance out of fear, many couples seem to abhor the work involved and choose to take what seems the easier route. We need to realize that no matter the reason for the avoidance, the problems do not go away. Even when we can avoid marital difficulties for periods of time, the underlying reasons for these difficulties still affect everything we do. Psychiatrist and author M. Scott Peck warns us of the consequences, explaining, "If all the energy to think seems troublesome, the lack of thinking causes far more trouble and conflict for ourselves as individuals and for the society in which we live."[2] The trouble and suffering Dr. Peck refers to definitely apply to the repetitive and unresolved problems in marital relationships and to the misery created by those marriages that fail.

The consequences of not thinking deeply about issues can be seen in all aspects of society, especially in the state of marriages today. Once again, M. Scott Peck concisely pinpoints this social problem. He emphasizes that "One of the major dilemmas we face both as individuals and as a society is simplistic thinking—or the failure to think at all. It isn't just a problem, it is the problem."[3] Underscoring the failure of any marriage is simplistic thinking on the part of one or both partners.

Reading, understanding and digesting the information in this book, therefore, will require work. The principles and ideas presented take courage to learn, follow and accept. However, the work, if done diligently, promises rewards. The primary reward is the possibility for a loving and productive relationship. For those who are married or are planning to get married, it is time to stop putting off the work. We owe it to our marriage partners and to our children. Most especially, we owe it to ourselves.

The Need for Understanding

It is estimated that 50 percent of married couples end up in divorce. Of the 50 percent who remain married, perhaps only half of these couples consider theirs a good relationship. In today's reality, only one in four marriages actually succeeds. Yet even with these intimidating numbers people continue to get married. They do so with the expectation that their relationships will be different. If approached properly, marriage can be the most productive and profitable challenge of our lives.

All couples start out on a positive note. Even if partners experience problems while dating, their commitment to each other is filled with hopes and dreams. So what happens to all these dreams and aspirations? The reasons typically given for the demise of marriages seem endless: changes in personality, boredom, alcohol, loneliness, midlife crises and affairs. Divorced couples echo these reasons for the collapse of their own marriages. The truth is, however, these are never the reasons. Nor are any of the other oversimplified explanations most people give for marriages that are failing or have already failed.

In my opinion, the typical explanations for the collapse of a marriage are actually consequences. As we will discuss later regarding each person's psychological lifestyle and the approach each person brings to problem solving, we often mislabel the real problem. Often I tell my clients about Jim, a high school student who was consistently getting poor grades. Most of his teachers remarked that Jim's problem was that he was lazy. In truth, this was not his problem but rather a consequence of a more severe underlying problem.

Jim perceived himself as being academically stupid and reached this conclusion in his early years of schooling for numerous reasons. He was always compared to his sisters who received A grades. Teachers told him he was nothing like the rest of his family. He did poorly in school, which reinforced his negative self-image. Ingrained with this self-image, Jim decided, albeit unconsciously, not to try very hard in the world of academics. In addition, he felt that if he did try, he would embarrass himself further. Thus the reason he was labeled lazy. But, as we can see in this situation, laziness was not the core of his problem; it was merely his solution.

Similar mistaken conclusions are often made in failed marriages. Lying beneath the reasons given for failed marriages, often below the level of consciousness, are the real problems that create the consequences. Just as a fever is a symptom indicating an underlying physical problem, so it is with the condition often cited for the failure of a relationship. Alcohol, boredom, affairs and the other cited reasons are all symptoms and consequences of more significant problems that are rarely and sometimes never addressed. Ignoring the real underlying problems often leads to the consequence of divorce.

Usually when a couple first comes into therapy for marriage counseling, one or both partners have long personal lists of what they consider to be the reasons for their poor relationship. One partner might explain they have grown apart and no longer have anything in common. The other might describe the ongoing arguments they have, even while admitting they are often over trite areas. A spouse might explain he or she is just tired of putting up with his or her partner's behavior and attitude. One spouse might complain his or her partner watches television all night or drinks a six-pack of beer or bottle of wine in one sitting. As partners describe in detail these and other reasons for marital strife, they presume these items of contention are the actual reasons—and the only reasons—for their marital problems.

As I brought up earlier, the actual problems in marital conflicts are deeper and more involved than the situational complaints expressed by couples in and out of therapy. The real causes for marital problems are not new to the marriage or even recent, as some couples may think. The underlying reasons for all problems in marriages were there from the beginning although the issues might have become more problematic or grown in intensity over time. Each individual in a marriage initially needs to learn, understand and accept this. In order to steer clear of the mistaken rationale often given for a failing marriage, we need to acquire a method for understanding the underlying dynamics of a healthy relationship as well as the underlying dynamics of an unhealthy one from a deeper point of view. From the beginning, all marriages have the potential to be healthy and creative as well as the potential to be unhealthy and destructive. The underlying reasons for either are within each of us and they have always been there. Part of the challenge is to discover these primary reasons that spell the difference between a successful and failed marriage.

Terry and Gerard's Story

Terry initiated therapy in her early forties. In her first therapy session, she came alone but explained she wanted her husband, Gerard, to attend eventually also. Midway through the first session, Terry described the marital situation that brought her to therapy:

> I was eighteen years old when we were married and Gerard was twenty. From the beginning of our marriage we have been living as brother and sister. I wanted to have children after two years of marriage, but Gerard kept putting the topic off. Since we were not going to have children at that time, it did not bother me that we were not intimate. I saw no point in having sex and Gerard never seemed to mind either. Twelve years have gone by and we still do not have children. I do not want to get a divorce; I do not believe in it. I know it might seem strange that I took so long to address this problem. I am both embarrassed and depressed about our relationship. It is even hard for me to be here.

Gerard came to counseling for a few sessions but talked around the issue of why there was not a physical relationship in their marriage. Soon he decided he did not need therapy. With Terry left to deal with the problem on her own, she began to discuss her background and the decision she made to get married. She explained that she spent most of her life in foster homes and was allowed to go out on her own at eighteen. While attending college, she met Gerard while getting her car repaired. She explained:

> Gerard was a car mechanic and seemed very concerned for my welfare. I was really taken with his concern. We started dating

and he asked me to marry him six months later. We eloped, because there was very little money. He fell asleep on our wedding night and, I really am embarrassed to tell you this, we didn't consummate our marriage until six months later. We argued a lot over this, but he kept saying he wasn't ready for children. I saw no point in having sex until we were ready to have children.

This is an obvious example of how marital problems are often present from the beginning. Neither Terry nor Gerard had any idea as to what a love relationship entailed. Gerard did not finish high school and worked at a gas station for two years before working on cars. He was a loner and never dated before meeting Terry. Having experienced six or seven foster homes since she was a child, Terry never developed an understanding of what a family or marriage entails. They married as two children taking on an adult challenge.

Terry completed college and was left to support the couple financially. Gerard drifted between jobs and spent most of his free time in the basement playing video games. Terry spent her free time reading, watching television or, as she explained, "Often, I fell asleep out of boredom." As the marriage continued without any changes, Terry finally reached her breaking point. During one of our sessions, she faced the reality of her situation:

> I know I have wasted a lot of years. I was too afraid to do anything about it. I never wanted to be divorced. As a result, I kept myself busy and ignored the reality of our relationship. I know we are both really immature. During the last few months of therapy, it has become obvious that I do not know how to have a relationship. Coming from my background, all I wanted was a family and children. I got married without any understanding of maintaining a marriage. This is not all Gerard's fault. He definitely has problems, but so do I.

Terry was open to spending more time in counseling. She wanted to reach an understanding about herself, realizing her background left her in a state of ignorance about many aspects of a healthy relationship.

She was interested in learning a philosophy that she could apply not only to herself but also to all the other adult challenges in her life. All of this would take time, but since Terry still had hopes of having a family someday, her enthusiasm to learn made the change a real possibility. Terry's need for growth may seem extreme, but we should not miss the point that it is crucial for all of us to understand that we all enter the state of marriage with some degree of ignorance.

Harold and Verne's Story

During his first session, Harold came across as melancholy and depressed and he explained to me his marriage had taken a toll on him. His wife, Verne, and he met after both were divorced. They had been married for ten years when Harold, now forty-two years old, finally sought counseling for himself and his marriage. Harold wanted to know if he was totally at fault, as his wife kept repeatedly saying. He explained:

> What attracted us to each other is now becoming annoying. Often I prefer to be by myself and I don't open up a lot. She has many friends and is out all the time or on the phone. I don't need a great deal while she seems to need a lot of attention from a lot of people. I admit to being a poor conversationalist and she complains that I never do enough. I am trying to make her happy, but she always seems to need more. I am totally worn out.

I asked Harold how long this had been going on. He said, "We dated for three years and that was very stressful and emotional. I guess since then." Harold explained he knew he and Verne were opposites when they married, but he thought it was good for him since he tended to be the quiet type. Harold continued:

> Three years ago I found out she was having an affair. I thought it had stopped, but now I think it is still going on. I don't want another divorce. So I ignore all the people she goes out with and constantly talks to on the phone. I don't think I can ever please

her; she needs so much attention. A few years ago, I decided to let her do what she wants. But it is getting more and more ridiculous. I can't take it if she is seeing that guy again.

Harold had tried resignation as a solution to his marriage. He sadly expressed, "I thought letting her do what she wanted would make her happy. Now she's just throwing more and more in my face." Harold didn't know what else to do to alleviate the tension.

Harold was very reserved and had a hard time expressing his feelings. He knew what he felt, but only shared his emotions with the help of another person prodding and prompting him. Harold feared the reality of his thoughts and feelings and the consequences if he ever listened to them. They all indicated a hopeless situation. In fear, he had decided to ignore as much as he could. As a direct result of his resignation, he had fallen into a deep depression. When I met with Verne, she did admit to having an affair but insisted she was only talking with the man now. She did not see anything wrong with maintaining a friendship with her former lover and said matter-of-factly, "I guess I need a lot of attention and I've lost feeling close to Harold. That's why I go out all the time."

Verne felt she did not need counseling. What I think she really meant was that she did not want or need to be confronted about her behavior. Harold adamantly did not want a divorce, yet he could not stand his marriage. Frustrated and depressed, not wanting to fight with his wife any longer, he returned to being resigned and discontinued therapy shortly thereafter.

Finding Your Life Philosophy

In order to accomplish the goal of discovering why some marriages succeed and others fail, we must start with a philosophy. Without a basic understanding of ourselves and of the dynamics involved in how we problem solve, we go through life unperceptive. It is as if we start out on a trip without a destination, map or sense of direction. Most psychologists would agree on the need for preparation. The psychologist Alfred Adler speaks of the consequences of omitting preparation when he emphasizes that "The greater number of failures in regards to sexuality, love and marriage can be traced back, as can all failures, to the lack of preparation."[4]

By acquiring a philosophy of human behavior and a method for applying it, one will be armed with a system to use in preparation for marriage and for the marriage itself. Using the philosophy as it is meant to be applied also holds the potential to bring back to life a relationship that seems to be slowly falling apart. Finally, if a marriage has failed, the use of an insightful philosophy regarding human behavior will pinpoint many of the actual reasons it did fail.

As you personally adopt this philosophy and apply it to yourself and your relationship with your partner, you will begin to find out there is always a common denominator underlying all behavior and all choices we make. This is not to say everyone has the same common denominator. Each couple is unique, yet all couples have one thing in common: There are always specific and definitive underlying reasons—the common denominator—for a marriage being healthy or unhealthy.

Most people, even when they are initiating therapy, are totally unaware there are underlying reasons why their marital problems either are resolved or continue to grow in intensity. Many make the mistake of focusing only on the presenting issue, the one that is causing the most discontent at the time. When problems do occur, couples tend to treat each incident as a separate entity. They do not see the common threads that run through the majority of their marital conflicts. Couples presume their present conflicts are the main problems and perhaps the only difficulties to be resolved. With this perspective, problems keep recurring. If a resolution is to be found to marital problems, this type of thinking needs to be corrected.

We need to realize it is always a mistake to examine any individual or marital problem in isolation of all the facts. When problems are handled without taking the full person into consideration, not only is it a waste of time, but also it can make things worse. Unless the root causes for a problem are dealt with, major underlying sources will never be brought to light. As a result, similar or even worse issues will come about in the future.

Think of it as trying to rid a lawn of weeds. If we only cut off the top of the weeds and remove all their leaves, it might look as if the problem has been resolved. We cannot see the roots of the weeds and therefore presume the lawn is now healthy. Yet, the reality is since the roots of the weeds were ignored, the weeds will reappear. When dealing with marital problems, the same holds true. The root causes always need to be addressed or the problems will continue to come back in one form or another. In the relationship between two people, the so-called "weeds" often appear early in the marriage. They are then often responded to inappropriately, never getting to the root causes. It may take years for the weeds to fully appear, but they usually do. When a marriage ends after twenty-five or thirty years, in essence, the roots of the couple's issues were ignored on an ongoing basis.

Kara and Mat's Story

Kara and Mat initiated therapy in their fourteenth year of marriage. They had a twelve-year-old son and a ten-year-old daughter. Both Kara and Mat agreed on the primary issue presently taking place in their marriage but were accusing each other for being at fault. The issue centered on the differences they had in parenting. Kara explained:

> Mat is always pressuring the children. He never lets up, especially with our son Tim. I think Tim is a good student and he loves sports. Mat is constantly berating him for not doing or trying enough. I can't stand the way he treats him. Tim idolizes his father but is afraid of him at the same time. I feel Mat is doing a great deal of harm to Tim. We argue about this all the time. It's reached the point where I think it is my responsibility to get Tim away from Mat.

Kara and Mat seemed to have a good relationship other than this parenting issue, which was driving them apart. They were both holding rigidly onto their belief systems regarding how their children should be raised. Mat, convinced he was right, explained his position and vehemently disagreed with how Kara handled things. He explained:

I feel Tim is a very talented kid. He can be a very good student when he wants to be and even his coaches agree he could be a better athlete if he made more of an effort. I just want the best for Tim and Kara doesn't seem to care. She drives me nuts on how she overly protects Tim. She treats him like a girl and thinks there is nothing wrong with him sitting around. Before we had children, I was totally in love with Kara. Now I am starting to resent her more and more. We never fought as much as we are now. Kara has no idea how hard it is out there. As a father, I refuse to allow Tim to face life unprepared.

Both Mat and Kara were sincere in their beliefs and loving as parents. They both wanted the best for their children but were at odds in what "the best" involved. Based on their intrinsic makeup, they were opposites in terms of what they valued and emphasized as being important. In reality, neither of them was totally wrong, but due to the extreme positions to which each adhered, they could not see the worthiness of the other's perspective.

Mat was the oldest child of four boys. As a high school and college student he wrestled and played football. Due to his success in sports and academics, he was able to get a full scholarship to college. After college he enlisted in the Marines and met Kara a few years after he left the service. His career as a salesman was very successful and he believed in a strong work ethic. He explained, "I believe you have to put everything into what you do. Otherwise, someone else will take your place."

Kara was the youngest of three girls. She explained, "I come from a very loving family. We always did a great deal together and my parents supported us in everything we did." Kara was a cheerleader in high school and majored in education in college. She expressed a strong commitment to teaching her young third grade students and loved the relationship she had with them. As she was speaking, I thought Kara was the type of teacher who created wonderful memories for all her students.

Kara and Mat were experiencing destructive and repetitive clashes during the last few years of their marriage, because they were dealing with their differences on a superficial basis. They were attacking each other's behavior, especially in terms of handling their children. As a result, they omitted getting to the root of the problem. Mat and Kara loved their children and wanted the best for them. During one counseling session I emphasized this as the starting point for discussion. Once they saw each loved their children equally they were able to see each other in a different light. After several productive counseling sessions, they were in a better position to see they were both correct but needed to learn the art of combining both their approaches.

Once they were able to see the worthiness of both parenting styles, the conflicts between the two of them lessened a great deal. Both Mat and Kara were parenting with two very different philosophies and both had merit. By getting to the root of their personal philosophies, they were in a much better position to work together as parents. We discussed their childhood experiences and how these experiences differed from each other. As a result, each saw life and its issues from a different perspective. They were also able to recognize how their approaches to life other than with their children were also areas that could lead to possible contention. In this sense, their learning experience in therapy was preventive.

The need for finding a philosophy of life applies to all of us, not just those people having marital problems or those who have sought therapy for another issue. Psychotherapist Alfred Adler makes this point regarding our personal development when he emphasizes the need for each individual "to understand his own picture of the world—a picture he built up early in childhood which has served as his private map, so to speak, for making his way through life—is an essential part of the cure."[5] One primary goal expressed in this book will be for you to bring the reasons behind your decisions—including the decision not to act—to a conscious state so you can understand from a deeper point of view your real nature and that of those you love.

Understanding this philosophy takes study and practice, including applying it to the daily events in your life. Sadly, many people prefer instant results that come easily and without much work. Psychiatrist and author

M. Scott Peck warns that by avoiding in-depth thinking and taking the time to do it, we run the risk of overlooking "various aspects of our lives that are desperate for attention until they become full-blown crises."[6] Most clients wait for a crisis and only turn to therapy when the crisis has reached a level of breakdown. The same is true when clients come in to discuss their marriages. A crisis has occurred—an affair, total boredom, grown apart—and the relationship might very well be in its last stages.

Once we make the philosophy part of our everyday thinking, including a part of our marital relationships, we will see issues in our lives differently. Our roles as parents will evolve from a different perspective. Friends and social situations will be interpreted with greater insight. Our careers, in terms of meaning and purpose, will be handled and understood from a different focus. The philosophy will give to us an entirely new outlook on our lives, most especially the relationship we have with our spouses. The philosophy consists of four primary steps—accept human vulnerability, stop denying humanness, identify vulnerabilities and respond to challenges as a couple. Let's consider and discuss each of these steps.

First Step: Accept Human Vulnerability

The philosophy begins with this premise: no human being fully has what it takes to handle all that life presents. We are neither Superman nor Wonder Woman. With all the things we need to learn about ourselves, this is initially the most crucial notion to understand and come to terms with regarding ourselves as human beings.

Bryon's Story

Bryon came to counseling right after having a major conflict with his wife Stacey. He explained:

> Stacey says she can't stand me any longer. She told me to go to counseling or else. I know I am not perfect, but there are things she does that really bother me. We have two young children and I think she could do a better job taking care of them. I think I should have some say in how she raises our children. I don't mean to criticize her. She is a great mother. But she could do some things differently.

I asked Bryon to tell me a few things about himself and Stacey. He praised his wife very highly for being intelligent and a hard worker. He stated, "She is very successful in business and makes more than I do. She is also more social than I am." Over the next few sessions, Bryon continued to praise his wife but started to include information about the fights they were having. Two different instances he reported represented a continuous theme in terms of the way he criticized her. He explained:

> Last week, on a very cold day, I thought she had dressed the children the wrong way. It was very cold outside and I told her that I thought she was stupid to let the girls go outside and play dressed in those clothes. It was similar to the night before. I said to her— she says I yelled—that she was crazy for not putting warmer pajamas on the girls. She went nuts on me after I said this.

Bryon did not have a clue as to what might be the cause for his constant criticism of his wife. Bryon was an only child who came to America when he was sixteen. He explained that he had a hard time fitting in and felt inferior to the kids in his class. After college, he had a difficult time keeping a job. Since he married he had been out of work three times. After a number of counseling sessions, Bryon began to see that he had an underlying sense of being inadequate. He recognized that this feeling was also present when he was younger. Reflecting on his relationship with his wife, he began to see how he felt inferior to his wife and inadequate as a husband.

Prior to counseling, he never addressed these feelings or he repressed them as much as possible. Without realizing it, criticizing his wife was a reaction to his perceptions about himself. His criticisms were attempts to bring her down to his level. In denial of his own feelings about himself, his behavior and communication with his wife had become more and more harmful to the relationship. With the help of counseling, he was able to admit to his own feelings of inadequacy and was able to recognize how it was dictating his behavior. Over his months in therapy, his relationship with his wife began to improve a great deal. Once he stopped allowing his feelings of inferiority to affect his behavior he became a more understanding and appreciative husband.

The premise of acknowledging vulnerabilities calls us to recognize who we are as humans. It entails conceding the reality that we are physically, mentally and emotionally vulnerable. Acknowledging and accepting this reality requires we come to terms with our strengths and limitations. As you will see, the denial of our humanness is what underlies most of the problems we have, including the problems we have interacting with our spouses.

The reason the first step is so important and vital is because every human being, albeit unconsciously, spends part of his or her daily life denying this reality. The basic reason we spend part of our lives in denial is because this one factor—our fragile humanness—is what causes anxiety, feelings of inferiority and feelings of being overwhelmed.

Second Step: Stop Denying Humanness

We have difficulty facing our own personal fears and vulnerabilities as we go through each day and face various challenges. Think for a moment about the various times you might have felt anxious or had inferior feelings about yourself. If you are like most people, you will also see the many times when you either repressed these feelings or made attempts to move away from the situation causing them. When we are unable to repress or avoid, we usually react defensively and allow the negative feeling to direct our behavior.

Stop thinking that there is something wrong with you when you experience anxiety or inferiority. One of the basic tasks is to be aware and accept the fact there is nothing abnormal about these so-called negative feelings; they are a part of our humanness. The avoidance and denial of these feelings is what leads to inappropriate behavior and eventually becomes part of a person's neurosis. In this book we will look at how the habit of denying humanness affects not only the manner in which we choose our marital partners, but also how we relate to our partners throughout marriage. This denial of our humanness is what underlies and becomes the primary cause for the failure of most marriages. It may take years to fully surface and materialize. In such circumstances, the consequences of denial were delayed due to the strength of each person's ability to repress, deny or avoid. Unfortunately, as some find out, this works only for a period of time. Spouses who have the courage to face their vulnerable feelings are not only freer to live more creative lives as individuals but also able to act as healthier spouses. This type of openness can enhance a marital relationship.

Marian and Joseph's Story

Marian and Joseph came for marital counseling in their twenty-third year of marriage. Neither had experienced counseling before and therefore both were unaware that we all have feelings of inferiority and vulnerability. They were viewing their relationship only in terms of how they were or were not acting appropriately with each other. Over their years of marriage, their conflicts had become more intense and a distance was growing between them. They wanted their marriage to work and wanted to avoid divorce.

After a few sessions together, I saw Marian and Joseph individually to assess the perceptions they had of themselves both in terms of strengths and limitations. Both of them were surprised to discover some of their major feelings of inferiority and the range of fears they were carrying around with them on a daily basis. They were also surprised to discover how much these feelings were influencing their behavior, especially with each other.

When they returned to couples counseling, both Marian and Joseph began to look at their interactions with each other from very different perspectives than before counseling. Marian discovered the reasons for her jealousy and why she often resented Joseph's popularity. Joseph's outgoing personality became a reminder to her of what she was not. Rather than dealing with her personal social fears, she took her resentment out on her husband.

Joseph discovered the reasons why he sought so much attention from outsiders and saw how he often ignored his wife in the process. He recognized that his obsessive need for an audience was a compensation for his fears of being inadequate. In a real sense, the audience took precedence over his wife. Dealing with these personal issues and others that came up during counseling enabled Marian and Joseph to renew the once solid relationship they had in the beginning of their marriage.

Inferiority feelings are personal. Most of us understand what vulnerabilities—such as fearing rejection, being left out, feeling unwanted, failing, being alone and being abandoned—mean but no one experiences all of these vulnerabilities nor do people experience any of them to the same degree. However, based on numerous experiences during the first ten years of life, each individual develops two or three primary fears. Once formed, a person has them for life.

These fears are like buttons. Each of these buttons carries the label of personal fears or vulnerabilities. The fears are firmly and permanently ingrained in our minds. For the rest of our lives, any event or interaction, especially a challenge, has the potential for "tapping" one or more of our fears. In terms of the marital environment—which is filled with challenges and problems to be resolved—there is the potential for each partner to be tapped numerous times in any particular week. How each partner responds to being tapped and how each partner reacts to feelings of inadequacy becomes highly significant in terms of having a successful or failing marriage.

There will be times, and for many partners it may be the majority of the time, when these fears lead to defensive reactions. It is the easiest way out and the quickest way to counter the fears. Our responses, once our fears are awakened, become the keys to whether we function as healthy or unhealthy human beings. In the marital relationship, the manner in which we respond and interact with our spouses when feeling vulnerable is of major significance when considering the difference between a healthy or unhealthy relationship.

As we look closer at the issues of the marital partners cited in this book and see how they respond to each other and to their marital problems, we will see the importance of knowing as much as we can about human vulnerability and the many ways we respond to these vulnerabilities. In order to enhance the chances of making healthy decisions, the first task for us all is to discover our vulnerabilities and to own them as our personal buttons. The second task is to discover our repetitive defensive solutions to these vulnerabilities. The best way to gain this insight into our mostly unconscious world is by working with a psychologist, especially one trained in cognitive-behavioral therapy. If this is not possible, there are areas one can investigate to gain knowledge of this psychological dynamic taking place within us on a daily basis.

Alfred Adler suggests four specific areas that are helpful in the exploration of emotional buttons: earliest childhood memories, dreams, especially those that are recurring, birth order position in the family and the primary issue with which a person is having difficulty at the moment. In the majority of cases, it is this primary issue or crisis that brings a person into therapy. In this last category a person has the opportunity to examine how a specific situation is awakening fears and creating anxiety and then to observe the response he or she has to these feelings.[7]

Early Recollections

Of the four areas Adler suggests for investigation, I, as a therapist, have always found the use of early recollections to be the most meaningful place to begin working with my clients. During the first few weeks of therapy, I ask a client to tell me his or her earliest recollection. I instruct my client, "Think back as far as you can and complete the sentence: I remember one time when…" Then I ask my client to share six or seven more recollections. Each recollection a client presents in our therapy sessions is a personal perspective on him or herself (positive and negative feelings) and a perception of the world in which he or she lives. Each recollection carries a wealth of information, including which vulnerabilities the client is most sensitive to and the perceptions the client has of his or her life and of the world around him or her.

Rocco's Story

Let's look at a client of mine who came for therapy at two distinct stages of his life. His story shows how our fears and vulnerabilities are with us for life and how they can influence decision-making at each stage of our lives.

When Rocco first initiated therapy at the age of twenty-seven, he was engaged and about to marry Kate, his girlfriend of three years. He explained he was experiencing periods of depression and had come to realize these feelings of depression were not new but something he had been trying to deal with since his teenage years. What Rocco did not realize was that his depression was not the primary problem. It was a consequence of the way he was thinking. As with many of his emotional experiences, the depression developed as a result of a distorted self-image. Because of his poor self-image, he often misinterpreted many of the experiences and interactions he had with others. Thinking the thoughts he was having about himself and others were true forced him into further depression.

He explained the depression seemed to be getting worse and lasting longer. He also stated, "My frustration and anger levels seem out of control and beyond what the situation deserves." He felt confident about his marital plans and said his future wife, Kate, was busy with all the preparations. After getting a good picture of Rocco's situation, I asked him for his earliest recollection and he shared: "I was about six years old and was going on vacation with my family. I come from a large family. Before my father got on the highway, he stopped to get gas. While he was getting gas, I went to the bathroom. When I came back, the car was gone. What made it even worse is they took a long time to realize I was missing."

Rocco's first recollection and all of our own recollections should not be interpreted to mean that one event makes us who we are. Hundreds and hundreds of experiences, large and small, go into creating our self-perceptions and the perceptions we have of the world. As we go through the early years of our lives, we go through the process of formulating these perceptions, both positive and negative. By our teenage years they become imprinted in our minds. As Adler emphasizes, "The first memory will show his fundamental view of life, his first satisfactory crystallization of his attitude."[8] The perceptions revealed in early recollections include the positive feelings about who we are along with negative feelings (inferiorities, fears and anxieties).

Early recollections are actually present tense. Even though the way I ask a client is in reference to his or her past, a client is actually dipping into his or her subconscious in the present where the memories are stored. Adler explains, "His memories are the reminders he carries about with him of his own limits and of the meaning of circumstances."[9]

It is not the event itself that is important. What is most significant is what the event tells about the person's perspective on himself and life. Remember, we develop perceptions about ourselves over years of development and reach conclusions from hundreds of experiences. The recollections, so to speak, put these perceptions in capsule form. As we can see from Rocco's first recollection, our fears and personal inferiorities are usually included in these memories.

In examining Rocco's first recollection, we can spot two major fears: the fear of abandonment ("the car was gone") and the perception of being insignificant ("they took a long time to realize I was missing"). In therapy, these insights are first seen as hypotheses until there is confirmation from other areas of investigation. Based on my personal experiences as a therapist, the conclusions made from early recollections are confirmed the majority of time when discussing areas such as dreams, the effects of birth order position and the manner in which the client interprets his experiences with other people.

Presuming Rocco's major fears are abandonment and feeling insignificant, we can begin to see how they operate in two primary ways. The first is his response to the daily events in his life, all of which have the potential to tap into one or both of these fears. For example, one day he was sitting at his desk at work and lunchtime was approaching. Three of his friends passed by his office on their way to lunch and did not ask him to come with them. Rocco's "insignificant" button was immediately tapped and he began to feel badly about the experience. We could say that many people would have this emotional response as a result of being left out and not asked to join friends at some event. However, because not all people have the same vulnerability, the feelings would not be as intense as Rocco's. When similar occasions began to pile up and Rocco continued to feel left out, the feeling of being down turned into a depression. Finally, what he does because of his sense of inferiority spells the difference between being healthy or not.

The next way these two fears affect Rocco's life is in the way he goes about making decisions, both large and small. Continuing the example of three friends who overlooked inviting Rocco to lunch, in the future Rocco might try doing everything he can to please his friends so as not to be ignored again. In other words, since he felt insignificant even prior to this experience, he takes the blame for being left out and therefore feels he must do something for it never to happen again. He will try to be "the ultimate pleaser" in order to gain their acceptance.

There is the possibility that Rocco's reaction to this and other similar events would make him angry. Unaware that one of his buttons has been tapped, he might take his friends' rejection as a personal affront. If he follows this path of thought, he might very well seek some form of revenge.

I often ask clients: "Knowing what you do about Rocco based on his early recollection, what type of woman would he date and perhaps marry?" If he allowed his choice to be primarily dictated by his fears—abandonment and insignificance—one might presume that Rocco would be attracted to a woman who showered him with attention. This might seem the most logical, since Rocco would not want his feelings of inferiority constantly being tapped. The problem is, however, that responses dictated by our inferiorities are not logical.

If Rocco was primarily directed by his feelings of being insignificant, he would have the need to constantly try to prove his self-worth. If a woman showered him with constant attention, his obsessive solution to be accepted would have nothing to prove. It is like a person who needs to win at everything for fear of being a loser. He would not choose easy competition since that would do little to satisfy his inferiority of being a loser. Therefore, without being conscious of how he is making this decision, Rocco would more than likely be attracted to an independent woman who showed her love intermittently. Since Rocco's primary life goal is to overcome his feelings of being insignificant, it is necessary that he have experiences where this button is tapped. In keeping his vulnerability alive, so to speak, his unhealthy solution is kept alive as well.

Rocco expressed in therapy that he was marrying Kate because she was attractive, fun to be with and smart. He said he loved Kate for her many upbeat qualities. These might be some of the reasons, but if Rocco was primarily driven by his fears of not being good enough, then his reasons for marrying were more complex. Based on his emotional need to overcome his insignificance, he would want to marry a woman who demanded he do just that. In other words, she might call into question his worthiness and challenge his significance in an unhealthy way.

During his first time in therapy Rocco reported having a recurring dream. All dreams are revealing, but recurring dreams are an indication that the dreamer really considers certain perceptions as highly significant. The dreams Rocco had were of a sexual nature where he was having relations with a woman. However, before he felt sure enough about himself to perform, he had to do something for her to prove his self-worth. It could be as small a task as changing her automobile tire or fixing her clogged sink. By virtue of the way Rocco perceived himself and his participation with Kate, he had to do something to gain her acceptance before he felt worthy of her and of lovemaking. Standing on his own, he did not view himself as worthy.

If Rocco did not correct this crucial mistake of allowing his inferiorities to dictate his choices, he would most likely marry a woman with a vast array of emotional needs. People consistently using their unhealthy solutions often are attracted to people also using unhealthy solutions. Initially Rocco might be satisfied in the relationship, because his solution was working and therefore his vulnerabilities would temporarily be overcome. Eventually, however, still trying to prove himself as worthwhile, he might say to a therapist after years of marriage, "I can never please her. She is constantly looking for more. Whenever I do or say something she does not like, all hell breaks loose. I have never been this unhappy." Unfortunately, Rocco had to end therapy due to his work schedule and the time needed for his marital preparations.

Rocco came to therapy for the second time when he was sixty-four. He had been married thirty-seven years and had one son and two daughters. He ran a successful private practice as a physician and was looking forward to the prospect of slowing down. The first time he entered therapy was because he was about to be married. The second time he was separated and sought help for depression. Kate had filed for divorce.

Rocco was well aware that there was ongoing tension throughout his and Kate's marriage. He knew the marriage had become one of survival that he was merely enduring as opposed to finding satisfying. The conflicts and hostility grew from year to year and had reached an apex during the last five years. Ironically, the conflicts turned from primarily marital clashes to vicious collisions with their children.

At this stage of his life Rocco had little regret for the impending end of the relationship. His sorrow and pain came with the loss of a dream. For most of his adult life he sought to have a family from which all wonderful things could flow. He so wanted not to repeat his own family history of marital discord and the history of so many others. As he explained when he returned to counsel with me, "I actually feel relieved. The craziness that was taking place in our house can now end, at least between the two of us." Rocco added, "The marriage was over years ago, with very little that was healthy about it. I was trying to keep the family together. I could never have left my children when they were young. But I also lacked the courage to admit my marriage was a wreck. Pathetically, I thought maybe one of us would die before the disaster of divorce."

There was no question Rocco was in a deep depression, coupled with anger on the verge of exploding. His tears flowed steadily during his first few months of therapy. His sadness was over the realization the dream was over. At one session he explained:

> I was not surprised at Kate's divorce announcement. She had been threatening divorce for years. It was her response to any conflict. It was as if she held me hostage, knowing I would do anything to keep the family together. In fact, the first time she threatened divorce we were only married a few months. It was over some minor disagreement, as in what color should the tablecloth be. The threats grew over the years and it was her way to resolve a disagreement. The tension was only absent when there was total affirmation of her needs and demands. The cost turned out to be more than money. To appease her, I lost myself.

Rocco expressed embarrassment as he went through the details of his marriage. He never pictured himself as being the castrated type. He was proud of his career as a physician and he loved the relationships he had with his patients. He was a proud father and actively participated in every area of his children's lives. To outsiders, Rocco, Kate and their children appeared to be the perfect family. What was taking place behind closed doors was another story. Rocco knew, through some close friends, that discordant situations like his were going on in many households and eventually many relationships ended after years of marriage. Both Kate and Rocco were interlocked in their neurotic solutions to life. Rocco felt the need to consistently prove his self-worth, while Kate continually demanded constant attention and admiration. There seemed to be no cure for the malignant state of their marriage.

Rocco's relief came with the knowledge that he was free to end his unhealthy solution to life. In hindsight, he regretted letting go of the wisdom he received from his first experience with therapy and choosing to ignore it. Or perhaps he did not understand it fully enough or realize how deeply it could function within a relationship. Rocco knew his buttons: the fears created by not being good enough. He lived in terror that this insecurity would cause his mate to leave him. And, in fact, he had been tortured by his wife constantly threatening to do just that.

Now that he could stand back and analyze the situation more clearly, something he was too terrified to do when he was married, Rocco could see how his actions kept reinforcing his neurotic need to please and be appreciated. He could also see how his behavior not only supported Kate's unhealthy lifestyle to always feel good about herself, but also fed and enhanced the severity of Kate's lifestyle.

One example, among many, that Rocco gave of his own fear of not being good enough and lacking the ability to be a good husband and father was telling:

> I have been making a good income for most of our marriage. After thirty plus years of marriage, it should have totaled in the millions. Kate and I are ending this marriage with absolutely nothing to show for it financially; we are in extreme debt. We moved several times when we did not really need to move. We bought and built houses above and beyond our means. We took trips and stayed in the best hotels, when there was no rational reason to do so. Expensive dinners were always part of the week, along with daily dips in an overheated pool and hot tub. And here I am only scratching the surface. My neurotic behavior went beyond just money.

With the strain and tension of always being in debt, along with the lack of admission that they were rarely satisfied for any length of time, both Rocco and Kate became what might be referred to as emotional enemies. It took Kate's seeking a divorce to stop the pathology between the two of them. However, the emotional tension between the two continued right up to the divorce settlement papers being received. Rocco summed up the lack of understanding in his marriage by describing a scene that took place just a week before the papers arrived. He explained, "Kate and I were walking toward the beach on a beautiful summer day. The water was blue-green and the temperature was perfect. Kate turned to me and said, 'Wouldn't you rather be on some beautiful island and at a resort than here at this beach?'" Rocco continued, "The really sad part of this story is even though I knew Kate's thought was crazy and just another want that demanded filling, I began to think of a way I could pull it off."

The discordant relationship of Kate and Rocco is just one example of why some marriages take a long time to end. Many marriages involve two people who lack the courage to come to terms with their individual demons; two people who lack the common sense to alter their ways of dealing with them. Rocco was unable to stop his addiction of proving himself worthy or to resolve his constant gnawing fear of being insignificant and inadequate. This was especially true given the environment of his marriage. Kate, who felt little self-worth, was stuck in her expansive need to have more and to do more. She was a woman who needed and demanded constant attention, no matter what the cost was to others. The pathology was there all along. It simply took years of marriage to reach its limit.

Dreams

The section on childhood memories reveals one technique for discovering the specific ways in which we experience inferiority and how we have created both unhealthy and healthy plans of action in response to these feelings. Exploring dreams is another significant method for gaining further information about these two areas of human experience and gaining more pieces to understand and see life's puzzle.

In the philosophies of Alfred Adler and Karen Horney, dreams are seen as one-act plays that are written by a person's perceptions and emotions. Any form of dream interpretation should never be done in isolation from the whole person. The thoughts and feelings that we have, both in our waking and sleeping states, must always be considered as a part of the whole. Each piece of information that we obtain about ourselves or others must only be evaluated as it relates to the entire individual.

Few would be foolish enough to examine one or two pieces of a one thousand-piece puzzle and come to a definitive conclusion about what the puzzle represents. In similar fashion, no one should be so naïve as to think he can reach a diagnosis of an individual by just looking at one part. All aspects of the individual, both in terms of quality and quantity, must be examined as part of one unit. Adler notes that if these parts are examined correctly, we will find that they do not contradict, but actually confirm one another.[10]

We are capable of having positive and optimistic dreams or dreams that are disturbing and frightening. However, it is best not to judge dreams as good or bad, even though our feelings when awake tell us differently. It is more appropriate to view the recalling of dreams as an opportunity to learn more about ourselves. Karen Horney advises, "In dreams we are closer to the reality of ourselves; that they represent attempts to solve our conflicts, either in a neurotic or a healthy way."[11] In other words, the solutions we have developed in response to challenges and problems remain the same whether we are awake or not. We will have some dreams where the feelings and drive toward our psychological goals will be more intense and powerful. In other dreams, we may experience feelings of fear and anxiety. In our waking states, we may not be aware of these feelings, but the dreams tell us it is so.

Dreams also can reveal the nature of our unhealthy solutions to our fears and vulnerabilities. In order to remain honest with ourselves as much as possible, it is always important to know that we are capable of being unhealthy. Dreams, if we remain open to their true meanings, can pinpoint the dynamics of our mistaken solutions. Dreams often present a problem to be solved, which in turn taps into one or more of our fears. We select a solution in the dream that is either one of courage or one permeated by caution and avoidance.

Adam's Story

In many situations we'll discuss one partner struggling in his or her attempts to respond to the neurotic needs of the other partner. The person may spend years in trying to do so with the fear that if he or she does not the marriage might end. Adam, married over thirty years, is one of these partners. He was reticent to consciously admit to the numerous times he was disappointed and frustrated in his relationship with his wife, Sally. While in these long stages of denial, he experienced many emotions which he repressed so as to continue his marriage. These emotions were revealed in many of his dreams. One dream's theme and content, although unique in itself, occurred many times during the last ten years of his marriage:

> I was taking Sally to a spiritual service. She wasn't too enthusiastic about going, but I was hoping she would like it. I was disappointed in the service and it wasn't what I thought it would be. Sally looked at me mockingly.
>
> It switched to where I was in my car; Sally did not get in. I had to get out and go look for her. I got lost in the basement of a huge building but finally found my way out. I tried to reach Sally by phone, but the dials kept falling off. People were watching and I was embarrassed. I was getting frustrated and angry about having to look for Sally. I felt she didn't care about how concerned I was that something terrible had happened and that I felt so unsure of myself in searching for her.

In counseling, the underlying goal of each session is to help the individual face life with more courage. By examining our dreams we have the opportunity to see the many ways we have developed responses to life's problems and challenges, including the challenge of marriage. If such information is used well, we can bring this knowledge into the waking state and hopefully make the necessary corrections in order to live a healthy life.

Adam had been frustrated with his relationship with Sally for many years. He knew it was no longer a loving relationship for either of them, but he still was willing to accept it for what it was. He knew the only way to keep the marriage intact was to please her in every way possible. This became more and more difficult during the later years of their marriage.

Sally mocked anything in which Adam was interested. Spirituality was one thing Adam could not give up, so he tried to win her over. Adam's dream showed how this was not working at all. The dream also revealed the separation between Adam and Sally, but Adam felt it was his responsibility to go after her so they could be together. The broken phone indicates how he was unable to make a connection with her and was embarrassed by his own behavior. Deep down he knew he was losing his identity. As he continually felt lost, his anger and frustration were increasing.

Adam was not surprised by the interpretation he and I reached, for he was finding it more difficult to deny the state of his marriage. His ensuing sessions would determine whether Adam could develop the courage to face the reality of Sally's lack of love and caring for him. It would also take a great deal of courage to get his identity back, even if it meant risking the end of his marriage.

Birth Order

The birth order position in a person's family and how that individual perceives his or her particular position is another technique for discovering the lifestyle we have developed as adults. The specific inferiorities and senses of limitations we have developed from childhood are significantly influenced by our interpretations of the positions we have among our siblings.

Each child, by virtue of birth order position, not only views and experiences his or her environment differently, but also is treated differently. Each child is born into a different situation by virtue of birth order and therefore interprets him or herself and his or her environment accordingly. In the majority of families, each birth order position is treated differently from the other positions in the family.

A helpful visual for understanding the effects of birth order is to imagine an oval running track. Each child is running, perhaps walking, around this track, but in a certain order. Their positions can be labeled first (eldest), second (middle child) and last (youngest). The eldest will be influenced not only by his position, but also by the movement of the others. The same holds true for the middle and youngest children. We will discuss some general characteristics and perceptions each person may assume as a direct result of his or her position in the family.

The Oldest Child

The oldest child is in a distinctive position. For a brief period of time he was the only one present and as a result most likely received a great deal of attention. But then the second child was born and the attention must now be shared. Adler notes this situation when he explains, "for a while he is the only child and sometime later he is 'dethroned.'"[12] The experience is considered unique, because the other siblings never have this experience.

The theme of dethronement is highly significant. Within a range of options, there are two strong possibilities regarding how this dethronement might affect the eldest child's perspective on himself and of his environment. One is that the eldest may spend a lifetime in his attempts to get the throne back and make sure he keeps it. There is also the possibility that the eldest child might become resigned to this experience and have little motivation for achievement or success.

In many family situations, the eldest will do everything to get his position back and to keep it. As a direct result of this striving, he will develop characteristics that will enable him to regain the top psychological position in the birth order. He will do everything to please authority figures in order to gain their approval, for it was in his relationship with them that he experienced the dethronement. He will have a tendency to be very organized and rules-oriented while realizing the importance of power and authority.

The eldest child often is driven to succeed in every area in which he chooses to function. He is very competitive and works hard at his talents in order to achieve success. Developing a track where he protects others and feels responsible for their safety is common for an oldest child. Even though there is nothing inherently wrong with these characteristics, Adler warns that "Even the striving to protect others may be exaggerated in a deep desire to keep those others dependent and to rule over them."[13] As an adult the oldest child is often found in a career of authority and power. In marriage the eldest is often the dominant figure in the marriage and perhaps the most conservative.

The Middle Child

As dethronement acts as a major consideration for the oldest child, having a pacemaker is one of the primary molding factors for the second born. How he perceives himself in ability and self-worth is greatly affected by the actions and abilities of the older sibling. In some cases, the second child may do everything in his power to catch up. As Adler explains, "He behaves as if he is in a race, is under full head of steam all the time, and trains continuously to surpass his older brother and conquer him."[14] Even though Adler uses the male sex in his reference, it should be noted that the gender of each sibling will also affect the perspective of each birth order position.

If the middle child has a different perspective on himself in this position, he may feel as if he has been slighted, the eldest getting and achieving more than he. With this attitude, he may try to achieve his psychological goals in the opposite way of the oldest. Rules and organization may be of no use to him. Rebellion of some sort is more than likely, such as taking shortcuts rather than following the rules. Adler warns, "Beware of his revolutionary subtleties."[15]

The Youngest Child

The youngest child has no one behind him, but he has many pacemakers. He might be pampered in some ways and end up using that for all it is worth. However, from another perspective, since he has all these models in front of him, he may become highly talented and competitive. Adler explains, "Because he is so much stimulated and has many chances for competition, he often develops in an extraordinary way, runs faster than the other children, and overcomes them all."[16]

If the youngest chooses his unhealthy solution, he will react more to be spoiled. As a result, he will lack true ambition and shy away from competitive situations. He may feel that others can do everything better than him, thereby emphasizing his feelings of being inferior.

Applying the birth order formula to marital relationships might present a difficult task, but it nonetheless should be considered an important variable to how each partner relates to the other. A great deal, of course, depends on how each partner has interpreted his or her position of birth and whether he or she has responded to it in a healthy manner or not. There are many variables to consider. Depending on the solution each person has brought into adult life as a result of birth order position, the solution will dictate what type of person he or she chooses to marry, how the marriage will function and whether the relationship has a chance to be healthy or not.

Neurotic Demands

In considering the unhealthy solution, there is always the possibility that an individual could function neurotically throughout his or her entire life without interference. A great deal depends on the strength of the neurosis, how well others cooperate with the neurotic demands and whether or not anything interferes with the rigid demands of the solution.

Often, these three categories are not met throughout most people's lives. More often than not, something occurs in an individual's life that derails the rigid solution and interferes with the exaggerated demands. This is especially evident when individuals or couples first come for counseling. It is very unlikely that a person comes to therapy without some sort of crisis. As a psychologist, I have never had someone say in the initial session, "Nothing is going on in my life that is a problem. I just want to get to know myself better." There is always an incident that brings a person to therapy. As Adler explains, "We must remember that it is the exogenous factor which sets the match to the fire."[17]

In marital situations, it is common for the exogenous factor to be an extramarital affair that has been exposed. It is often the case that a suspicious text message or e-mail sent by one partner was discovered by the spouse. In other situations, the exogenous factor could be a major or sudden illness that has occurred in the family or a financial crisis that is threatening the loss of everything. It could be that one partner is becoming more and more neurotic in his or her demands, thus creating further havoc in the marital relationship. Finally, one partner may see the sickness in the relationship and seek help. This occurs many times in marital therapy where one partner comes to therapy expressing he or she can no longer survive in the marital environment as it presently stands.

No matter what incident an individual or married couple brings to therapy, it is always important to examine it closely in terms of how it affects the person's typical solution to life's problems or how the event affects the marital relationship. As with the use of dreams and early recollections, each factor must be considered in relation to the entire person. It is the exogenous factor that has somehow interfered with the person's lifestyle goals and as a result has awakened previously hidden feelings of inferiority and inadequacy. By examining how this factor has occurred and how it has affected each marital partner, further insight will be attained in the exploration of each person's neurotic solution. At the same time, it will bring further knowledge to how the couple has, for perhaps years, been living under the shroud of a nightmare.

Mark's Story

Mark came to therapy when he was sixty-two years old, married for thirty-nine years and had five children. He came for individual counseling, but he primarily wanted to discuss his marriage. During the first session he explained, "Our marriage has not been good for a long time. We exist together in the same house, but there is no real communication. We never have sex and that part of the relationship has never been good. Now, I am in the middle of a crisis and I cannot take it any longer. I am imperfect, for sure, but my wife seems to be getting worse and worse."

During the ensuing sessions, Mark talked about how he knew his marriage, at least a marriage the way it should be, was over for a long time. He never spoke about it to anyone hoping that he could just somehow work it out. With a tentative voice, he summed up his view of the marriage:

> The most important thing to me in my life is my family. My children have been a great joy to me. The biggest problem is keeping my wife happy. As my children got older and the situation became worse, they began to notice my behavior with their mother. Almost every day I took on the task of making sure she was not angry with someone, especially with one of my children. She was usually dissatisfied with me for one thing or another, which I accepted, and I chose to protect the children from her consistent negative reactions.

Mark explained how his wife could not stand any form of criticism or any situation that did not put her on a pedestal. He and the children learned how to deal with her narcissistic behavior. Mark acted as a buffer between his wife and his children and silenced his children's complaints about their mother's anger and cruel statements. Eventually, Mark realized his actions were telling his children "to do the same sick thing I was doing. I was indirectly asking them to save the family at all costs, even if it meant that we had to take turns fielding her anger, her unhappiness and her need to be the center of attention." He continued to reveal:

> I have realized in the past two or three years that I can no longer be a buffer. Rather than directing most of her anger to outsiders, it is now involving the children more and more. I tried to hide their mother's sickness of never being satisfied and always needing to be treated as number one. Now she is viciously going after one of the children for a certain period of time and then goes on to another. I always have one or two of my children sobbing to me about how she is treating them. I cannot let this go on any longer or I will actually lose my children in the process. If I allow this to go on, the only healthy thing is for them to get as far away as possible. I cannot let my wife do this to them or to me.

Mark was filled with a range of emotions, from anger to sadness to a dark depression. He was trying to keep his dream alive for years and now it was crumbling. He realized he should have done something about his marital situation years ago but was too frightened about the possible outcome. In Adler's terminology, it was the exogenous factor that forced him to take action. The match to the fire that Adler speaks about was his wife's cruel behavior now being directed at the children. Even though she continued to expect total loyalty to her and for him to take her side against the children, Mark knew this was one demand for loyalty he could not keep.

The marriage ended with nothing resolved. Mark remained in therapy to get help with another major task ahead of him. He explained, "She is good at what she does. She has now divided the children against one another and some of them against me. She makes up stories and distorts the truth so some of the children will stay loyal to her. As bad as things are right now, I am hopeful that things will come around someday with them. For now, I am free of her and I can now be a better father and love my children in a healthier way."

If it were not for the exogenous factor occurring in Mark's life— the attacks on his children—he might still be desperately trying to keep the marriage and family together.

Third Step: Recognize Unhealthy Behavior

No one likes feelings of vulnerability. They involve fear, inadequacy and a sense of inferiority. They make us feel uncomfortable and anxious. Because we are so uncomfortable with ourselves, we begin to develop a negative attitude about ourselves as well. Many of these inferior feelings are often distorted and the conclusions we reach about ourselves as a result of experiencing inferior feelings begin to eat away at self-love and self-respect. Due to this mistaken mind-set, we start to look for a way to nullify these feelings as much as possible. This is where we begin the process of trying to be free from all forms of personal discomfort and to search for ways to eliminate them. All forms of vulnerabilities that create anxiety force us into protective modes, resulting in the "shrinking" of our true selves and retreating from a complete and honest understanding of who we truly are.

The process of trying to create a method to avoid vulnerable feelings begins in the early years of our lives. During the first ten or twelve years of life, children try out all kinds of solutions. Some attempt to control as much as they can. Some opt to let others have the responsibility. Still others refuse to take anything seriously or treat things as jokes to avoid feeling vulnerable. And then there are those who overly emphasize the cognitive process as a means of denying or avoiding all feelings. Finally, there are people who avoid as many challenges as possible so as to limit the possibility for being tapped. Depending on a person's perception of himself and what he feels he is capable of, the personal solution takes on its unique form by the teenage years.

Psychoanalyst Karen Horney clearly describes specific categories of solutions one can develop in response to feelings of anxiety and inferiority. The two we will discuss and apply to marriage and the manner in which we relate to our partners are the expansive solution and the self-effacing solution. Each solution has as its primary goal to idealize the self rather than self-actualizing and working with who we truly are. This is what neurosis or our unhealthy solutions are all about: an attempt to deny part of our humanness and become something we are not. Everyone has neuroses that must be realized and dealt with if they are ever to have a chance to make healthy decisions. In the marital environment, the challenge for us all is to recognize our own personal neuroses and identify when we are using them in response to marital interactions.

While discussing these solutions, we need to keep in mind that no one totally uses just one solution all of the time. However, depending on our personalities and backgrounds, we have a tendency to favor one specific type of solution, convinced it is the one that works best for us. The solution we eventually choose operates at varying levels of intensity. Some people use their typical solutions 20 percent of the time (mildly neurotic), while others may use a solution 50 percent of the time (moderately neurotic). There are some who may even use a solution 80 or 90 percent of the time (severely neurotic).

We will typically see that a person chooses one of these solutions and then marries someone who is using the other. Both partners opting for the same solution creates too much conflict in problem solving.

Opposite solutions attracted to each other is perfectly normal and, in many ways, allows for different perspectives on the issues needing attention. It does become a problem, as we will see in future case studies, if one or both partners are too rigid in their use of any particular solution.

In reading through the description of each solution, it is each partner's responsibility to identify the solution that most applies to him or her when he or she is feeling vulnerable and attempting to respond to a challenge or problem. Studying the characteristics of each solution is also extremely helpful in understanding the solution most used by our partners.

We can presume that we use our defensive solutions at various times throughout our marriages. It may be difficult for a partner to admit to his or her neurotic solution, especially when a conflict is taking place. However, if each partner can at least admit to being imperfect, both partners can reach the perspective that by owning up to one's solution there is a chance not only to be personally healthy, but to have a healthy marriage as well. For either partner to avoid this admission puts the relationship at risk. By understanding the reality of this potential in our own marriages—lying about our true feelings—we enhance the possibility for having a healthy relationship versus one that is based on the selfish act of protecting oneself.

The Expansive Solution

This solution is called expansive because this is exactly what an individual does when choosing it. He is unable or unwilling to accept his real self. Part of the real self experiences fears and vulnerabilities, a reality the expansive person desires to ignore. In this denial, he actually expands or exaggerates who he is and what he can do in order to compensate for the limitations and the vulnerabilities he has. He creates an idealized image in an attempt to become more than human and even god-like. It is as if the person choosing the expansive solution is saying to himself, "If I can reach my particular psychological self-image, I will no longer feel inferior or vulnerable."

As with all possible solutions, the expansive solution has numerous variations and characteristics. No one person is totally expansive, but some people use this as their neurotic solution more than others. The expansive solution, when rigidly used, serves one main purpose: to move away from and to avoid all feelings of vulnerability and inferiority.

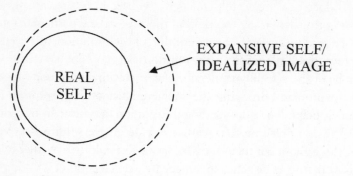

The expansive person's goal is to feel and be seen as superior, to be seen as the best in what he does. This goal becomes his neurotic demand so neither he nor anyone else will see his imperfections. The expansive person, by endless bragging and exaggerated boasting, inflates his sense of self to a nauseating proportion with the hope no one, including himself, will recognize any limitations. Once you know the expansive person and understand his obsessive goal, his behavior becomes predictable. Understanding the purpose of the underlying behavior helps to understand our partners and ourselves from a different perspective.

In order to move toward this fictional image and away from vulnerable feelings, there are certain personality characteristics an expansive person will acquire and those he will avoid because they are of no use. By knowing a person's goal and idealized image, we can understand the purpose and rationale for the manner in which an expansive person displays these characteristics and how they are utilized in his behavior. Recognizing the characteristics and types of behavior each solution reveals is very helpful in a marital relationship when each person is trying to understand not only his or her own behavior, but his or her spouse's behavior as well.

For expansive people, also referred to as narcissists, their so-called ideal is to achieve control, power and dominance over events and people. They demand to be adored and honored unconditionally and are always looking to impress people, even if it means distorting the truth. Narcissists are all about the "I" and, therefore, caring and having feelings for others are seen as secondary or unnecessary to their solution. As Horney explains, "Love, compassion, considerateness—all human ties—are felt as restraints on the path to a sinister glory."[18] If love or caring is expressed while on this track, it is not genuine, nor is it as intrinsically felt as one might assume. This is primarily true if a person is using this solution in the extreme. He may come across as being very loving, but there is always a catch. Those he loves must admire him first and foremost.

The expansive person's neurotic and rigid solution will become easily recognizable if one dares to question his point of view. Surrounding people might very well experience his explosive anger or rage. This not only happens between spouses, but also is not an unusual occurrence between a therapist and a narcissistic client.

In addition to lacking empathy for others, the expansive personality—depending on how much he is using this solution—is seen as bluffing his way through life. He is often empty inside and is more concerned with intimidating others than with his own personal growth or the growth and well-being of others. The expansive, therefore, must copy characteristics from others in order to obtain his honor and glory. Any feelings of real self-worth are temporary and must be reinforced on a regular basis.

This type of person often comes across as having a great deal of confidence and is often seen as charming, outgoing and in full control. Underlying this air of confidence, however, lies a very competitive person who always has to come out on top. He is a person who needs to continuously prove his self-worth, even if it is at the expense of others. This person cannot tolerate anyone who achieves more than he does nor accept someone who challenges his superiority. He will attach himself to people in power only if it serves the purpose of giving him more power. In most cases, he will involve himself with people who are beneath him and who are willing to consider him a hero.

In a marriage, an expansive person always prefers to be in the driver's seat. His or her marriage lacks true love, because it lacks respect for the other partner. Because an expansive person is so intent and driven to avoid all fears and vulnerabilities, his life is more about himself than his partner. Love is not valued, certainly not as much as personal success and the attainment of adoration. When the expansive person brings his solution into a marriage, it is never about achieving an I-you-we scenario. It always operates from the I-we position, where the *you*—the partner's *I*—gets little consideration.

Some degree of expansiveness is healthy. We need to reach beyond our real selves (expand) and dream of what could be. Fantasizing beyond the real self can lead to great acts of creativity. However, if a marital relationship is to be successful, it can never be the primary solution to either partner's life. When it is used too much, it destroys not only the real self of the individual, but also the possibility for having a loving relationship.

Walter's Story

As he was approaching his mid-fifties and the twenty-fifth year of his marriage, Walter began therapy with me, his eighth marriage counselor. He explained he was willing to try one more time. Unfortunately, his eighth counseling experience was to become a repeat of the first seven experiences. Due to massive issues of personal inferiority, Walter was unable to focus on his own issues. As with any neurosis, he sought to resolve his lack of self-worth in every arena in which he was operating. In therapy, the marital arena became a primary focus of attention. Throughout his years of marriage to Samantha, all issues centered on him and how he felt. He used every marital interaction as a test of whether he felt appreciated and honored for the person he was.

Walter's parents died when he was very young. He was passed around from one relative to another, always sensing—even told occasionally—he was never wanted. As a child, he felt berated and criticized and lived under the fear of never being wanted or appreciated. Entering his adult life, Walter was obsessed with anything that reminded him of his tortured past. He saw the world as threatening and hostile. With a narcissistic solution, he sought to counteract his fear of being unwanted with obsessive demands to be treated as number one by all around him, especially by his wife, Samantha.

Consistently being tormented by his lack of self-worth, Walter never believed Samantha loved him for who he was. Since he lacked self-love, meaning the ability to accept his real self, he could never believe he was lovable. Similar to how he perceived past relationships, he also felt alienated from Samantha and lived in fear of her rejection and abandonment. In an attempt to overcome these fears, he saw each event in his marital life as a test of whether he was appreciated and considered important. Any event or interaction between Samantha and himself that fell short of fulfilling his psychological and emotional demands aroused his anger and lead to another marital conflict. These ongoing situations grew in intensity from year to year. No amount of therapy could break his need for superiority. This marriage of twenty-five years would end only if Samantha reached the point of not being able to deal with it any longer.

While Walter admitted to being unhappy, he was not able to accept any personal responsibility for it. He blamed his wife and the lack of respect he perceived she showed him. This became his one and only issue. His life was all about him. Anything or anyone who fell short of honoring and respecting him became the enemy. In acts of desperateness, he made his marriage a living hell, as he demanded from Samantha total allegiance to him in every way imaginable. He was terrified to face any possible faults or limitations, for it only reminded him of his self-hate, the part of him that was unwanted. Due to his rigid narcissistic thinking and the degree of his rigid solution, Walter's eighth marriage counseling experience also ended in failure.

The Self-Effacing Solution

In the previous section, we saw how some choose the expansive or narcissistic solution to avoid as many negative and inferior feelings as possible. However, dictated by the manner in which a person perceives him or herself, many people choose the self-effacing solution.

Where the expansive solution has control as a goal to counteract inferiority, the self-effacing solution has the demand to be loved, wanted and accepted. It is as if the person choosing this solution is saying, "As long as I am loved or accepted, I am no longer inferior." Where the expansive person is in the driver's seat, the self-effacing personality sits in the passenger seat. Where the expansive person seeks to be superior and independent, the self-effacing person subordinates him or herself to others and becomes dependent, behaving as if he or she is helpless. Horney explains, "What he longs for is help, protection and surrendering love."[19] Compared to the person choosing the expansive solution, the self-effacing person does the exact opposite as he or she faces the various problems and challenges of life.

In order to achieve the goal of approval and fulfill the need to be taken care of, the self-effacing person must develop personality characteristics that will enable him or her to be successful in this solution. The goal to be accepted and loved influences the development of specific characteristics. To succeed at this goal, the self-effacing person becomes very needy yet caring. In almost everything he or she does there is the underlying desire to be accepted and loved by others, with the hope of counteracting his or her own feelings of inferiority. Emphasizing fear of failure and lacking any confidence in his or her assets, the person using this solution places him or herself in the shadow of someone else. Feeling insecure and incompetent, the person's aim is to be taken care of, thus avoiding responsibility for how things turn out. In order to accomplish this fictional goal of constant approval and acceptance, Horney explains the self-effacing person comes across as "the ultimate of helplessness, generosity, considerateness, understanding, sympathy, love and sacrifice."[20]

At first, such traits may seem admirable. Should we not all be about love? However, the self-effacing love is not actually true love, just as the expansive personality is not truly confident. In both cases, the love expressed by one or the air of confidence expressed by the other actually serves the selfish and defensive purpose of not having to deal with feelings of fear and inferiority. Once again, we can see the opposite nature of these two solutions when Horney speaks of the dependent personality as a "person who holds himself down to the extent of shriveling in stature in order to avoid expansive moves."[21] Compare this self-effacing diagram to the previous expansive diagram and see how they are directly opposite solutions.

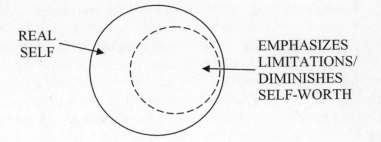

REAL
SELF

EMPHASIZES
LIMITATIONS/
DIMINISHES
SELF-WORTH

Samantha's Story

Samantha was married twenty-five years to Walter, whom we discussed in the section on expansive personalities. After years of marital therapy, she started attending therapy sessions on her own. She stated that she wanted her marriage to work but felt that no matter what she did she could not please her husband. She explained, "I want to communicate with him without worrying he might explode. He criticizes everything I do and says that I never think about him. I can never please him."

Samantha had a very easygoing nature and came across as loving and caring. However, as in all unhealthy solutions, there was an underlying reason for her demeanor. She was very sensitive to all forms of criticism and had a fear of conflict. She revealed growing up in the shadow of her sisters who, as she explained, "were more competitive and successful." In her early years of schooling, she fell behind her classmates academically and had a hard time making friends due to her shyness. Feeling her sisters were more pleasing to her parents, she sought her parents' love by being the good and obedient child.

During her teenage years, inferiority feelings continued to influence her behavior. She sought acceptance from one particular friend at a time, allowing that friend to dictate her daily activities. She developed a fear of authority figures and did what she could to please them in order to avoid rejection or even their possible wrath. During her teens, she had little respect for her own thoughts or desires and learned to accept her second-class position as a form of safety and security. Her overt acts of kindness and giving of herself in every way became the means for her to gain acceptance and love.

In early adulthood, with the fear of standing out and on her own, she was attracted to partners she felt would take care of her and protect her from all her fears. This excessive need, along with an extremely poor self-image, directed her to Walter, a marital mate under whose domination and direction she would have to live. Without realizing the consequences of her lifestyle choice, she put herself in the marital position where she would have to prove constantly she was acceptable, loving and loyal. Her lifestyle solution and sense of being a worthy person was totally dependent on the love and acceptance of her mate. This solution was quite evident in her interactions with Walter where she was at the mercy of her husband's approval and acceptance. Without major changes in each of the partner's solutions, the marriage was doomed to be neurotic.

Samantha knew she had to do some work on herself or face the reality of living in a draining and humiliating marriage. She also realized, especially after years of marriage counseling, that Walter was not going to change. To put herself in a healthier position, it was up to her to change. She came to realize that divorce was the only solution and the only opportunity for her to be healthy. Fear, however, was still holding her back. Samantha explained, "My family and friends will be shocked that I am ending a marriage after all these years. I never thought I would be in this position and certainly most of our friends presume our marriage is a good one." She then added, "Perhaps if they knew what was really going on between us, they might be more shocked that it took so long."

No solution an individual chooses should be considered better or worse than another solution. They are just different. As we've discussed, the solution any one of us opts for is simply one that is a better "fit" for us, while a different solution is better for another. In order to be healthy, we have the responsibility to identify our neurotic solutions and be ready to admit when we use them as responses to life's challenges. This awareness is especially mandatory when we respond to the challenges of intimacy and in our relationships with our spouses. We are on our neurotic paths when we are using our partners to fulfill our need to counteract inferiority (i.e., we have to be loved or have to control and dominate).

When a person is not governed by fear and vulnerability, he or she is flexible and not rigidly set in one solution. The person is able to respond to the challenge or problem at hand, rather than focusing on personal vulnerabilities. When we obsessively use one solution, it is a definitive sign the fears of inferiority are dictating our lives. Flexibility or being open to using the solution that is more appropriate at the time is a sign we care more about solving the problem or responding to the challenge than protecting our own selfish concerns. When a problem or challenge occurs, a healthy person is not controlled by his or her inferiority, even when such feelings are experienced. A healthy person is psychologically free to address a particular challenge and decide which solution will work best for him or her and for all who are involved.

It is when one or both partners lack this flexibility that the marriage becomes troubled. Rigidly staying with one solution is a clear sign that one or both partners are protecting themselves from personal vulnerability rather than responding to the challenge at hand. When this is the case in any marriage, the arguments become redundant and always end without a solution.

Brad's Story

Brad, now in the thirty-second year of his marriage to Amanda, came to therapy on the advice of his daughter. He was honest enough to admit that he probably would not have come on his own. He revealed:

> I am afraid to face the facts. If I face the reality of my marriage,
> I know it has to end. From my perspective, not my wife's, it has
> become a matter of just surviving with as few conflicts as possi-
> ble. I hate the person I have become and wonder how much
> more I can take. She is driving every ounce of joy out of me. I
> cannot remember the last time we laughed together. I know a
> number of my friends are divorced, but I never thought I would
> be in this position. I thought somehow I could get through it. I
> have come to therapy not for my marriage. I need help in doing
> what I have to do.

Brad knew a great deal about himself from a psychological point of view. He had gone through therapy in his early thirties, which he described as a great learning experience. He explained:

> I think I know a lot about how and why I am living this way. I am coming to find the realizations embarrassing and pathetic. In my past therapy, I learned a great deal about the effects of my childhood. I thought I had moved on and was writing another chapter in my life. What I cannot stand is what I have now finally come to realize. It is both shocking and something I find disgusting about myself. Not only did I not move away from my childhood experiences, but also I repeated them almost to a tee.

Brad was born to an extremely dysfunctional family. As a middle child of three, he had absolutely no relationship with his alcoholic father; no one in the family did, including his mother. There were times when there was tension and fighting, but for the most part their family life was empty and devoid of any kind of interaction. This was also true among the siblings.

Brad grew up very unsure of himself and never felt as if he belonged. Even though he played for hours with friends at one sport or another, he never had a sense of fitting in or being truly connected in any relationships. He sought acceptance in almost everything he did, but the relationships always seemed short-lived and ended as quickly as they began. The one relationship he worked on the most was with his mother. Not realizing it as a child, it was a relationship filled with pathology. He told me:

> For my mother, love was situational. One never knew from day to day whether there would be signs of affection and acceptance or actions of anger and rejection. My mother was an extremely unhappy woman who demanded from others their total commitment and loyalty. It was not love she was seeking but more allegiance and adherence to her way of thinking. She was a big, strong woman, sometimes physically abusive and more often than not emotionally cruel. She held the key to my feeling wanted or accepted. She opened and closed this door without logic or care.

Understandably, Brad did not fully realize the impact his childhood had on him. Brad viewed mothers as the affirmers of life. Well into his teenage years, Brad sought his mother's love and attention. The problem was that there was no consistency to the little love that may have been there. Through his actions and his words, he sought to be the good son. However, no matter what he did, it was never enough. Where there were victories, she spoiled them. Where there were failures, she made sure he never forgot.

Brad's mother often went days without talking, her eyes filled with anger and rage. Brad often presumed he had done something wrong but never had a clue as to what it might be. During these times of silence, he wrote letters to his mother promising he would be a good boy and seeking her forgiveness. Her response to these hopeless notes was simply, "We'll see." In addition, he gave her every dime he made, whether it was from hours of snow shoveling or caddying two loops a day. Brad was not sure if he did so thinking this is what a son should do or if she demanded it as part of a ransom for love. In either case, he translated actions such as these to mean he was worthwhile.

Brad thought he had let go of this childhood of discontent. He had married a woman he loved and whom he presumed loved him. He raised a family based on encouragement, support and, of course, love and affection. His wife and children never had to wonder if they were loved.

For the greater part of Brad's adult life, he felt he had gotten past all the sadness and trauma. He had every intention of being the best husband and father he could be. Little did he know, as his marriage continued on in years, he was falling back more and more into the role he once lived as a child. He did not totally blame his wife for their relationship reaching the unhappy state it was in, for he knew he was also responsible for letting it happen.

The first decade of marriage seemed to be calm. There were the normal ups and downs but nothing that was not easily resolved. The second ten years went well, but signs of what was ahead began to appear. Brad's son excelled in sports and Brad loved attending all the games and watching his son play. Amanda was upset at the attention Brad was giving their son and often mocked Brad.

Brad explained a similar situation that took place years later, but this time with his daughter. He was also proud of her and the woman she had become. Graduating from a prestigious and academically difficult college, she was doing momentous and meaningful work as a social worker. When out with his wife, Amanda, and friends, Brad often boasted about his daughter's work and related the wonderful conversations he had with her. The ride home alone with Amanda was always a disaster. She screamed, "What's all this crap about social workers? You think that profession is so great! You talk of your daughter as if she is something special. I think you have an odd relationship with her. Maybe something is going on."

During the last ten years, scenes like these came with more consistency and with increased venom. Could his wife, Amanda, actually be jealous of her children? Brad always knew Amanda needed and demanded more attention than what might be considered normal. Praise and admiration, without an ounce of criticism, was required in order to keep her happy and retain the peace. One mistaken word—mistaken in her perception—and there was a price to pay.

Then there was the game of silence. If she felt criticized or the attention was not coming her way, days of angry silence followed. Any attempt to talk was shunned or was listened to with the expectation of an apology. Brad explained, "This is when the letter writing began. I apologized and asked for another chance. During the times I tried to verbally say it, Amanda told me to put it in writing. So another letter was put forth." With a deep breath, Brad added with a degree of embarrassment, "Yes, I know. I did this at another time of my life."

One evening in therapy, Brad came in with another emotional letdown. Due to the economy, Brad's business was down and he had tried to discuss the situation with Amanda. Brad said she got angry and repeatedly yelled, "You must be doing something wrong. If you act in business the way you are here, no wonder it's failing." Brad commented, "I am positive she is impossible to please and absolutely sure our marriage will always be about her."

The final conflict arose from the relationship with the children.

Some call it the empty nest syndrome, but Brad knew it was much more than that. When the children were very young, they spent a great deal of time with their mother. Even when they became older they still visited on a regular basis. Eventually, it came to a point in their lives, as it should be, when their time was taken up by careers and their own families. Brad expressed with a great deal of frustration and with a voice of hopelessness:

> All of this did not sit well with my wife. She is angry the attention is going away from her. She will never admit this, for she feels her anger is justified. Amanda has never admitted to a wrong and I expect she never will. During the last few months she has had the audacity to say to me, "Your children do not love you anymore. Look how they are acting. What makes you think they love you?"

Brad did repeat history. It took him decades of marriage to Amanda to see it clearly. As things turned progressively worse and the pit of doom became deeper, Brad felt he could no longer live this way. He could no longer sit back and watch his children being treated in the exact same way he had been. It took him more than thirty years to fully see the light, but Brad still felt young and felt that joy was still a possibility.

Brad was saddened by the outcome of his marriage but hopeful about his future. He now fully realized he was raised by a mother filled with narcissism and he had unknowingly repeated the relationship with his wife. Starting out the marriage with a fairly good sense of self, he had become more and more self-effacing as the marriage went on. It would take courage to take the first step and to begin anew.

Fourth Step: Respond to Challenges as a Couple

All couples must learn to accept the fact that it is natural to have problems. As either a husband or wife, we can expect that our lives, if lived to the fullest, involve dealing with challenges. Given this reality, it is also natural we will often feel inadequate and inferior. We worry about failure. These feelings are perhaps most evident in the challenges inherent in the life of a love relationship. As spouses go through life together, both experience their own humanness and vulnerability as they respond to the challenges of parenting, financial issues and social norms, to name just a few.

In the majority of problem-solving situations in marriages, it is a tremendous advantage to have both solutions available. When dealing with a specific problem, one partner will most likely experience specific emotions and thoughts that will be different from the other partner's. As a problem surfaces, each partner will also have a different perspective on the problem to be resolved and each partner will experience different feelings of vulnerability. These differences present a tremendous opportunity in problem-solving. It is during these times when we can apply the trite but true statement that two heads are better than one. By appreciating each person's perspective and approach to a challenge, partners can work together in deciding which solution will be best in a particular situation.

For the purpose of clarity, we can divide life's challenges into five distinct categories. The first is the challenge of marriage and family. The second is our careers and work environments. The third is our social lives, the types of friends we have and our interactions with them. The fourth is the challenge of our individual selves, coming to terms with who we are and attempting to continually grow and develop. Finally, there is the challenge of discovering meaning and purpose in our lives. Some people include the challenge of spirituality with the fifth category. This final category actually permeates the first four challenges as we try to find meaning and a spiritual purpose in all aspects of our lives.

When taken seriously, challenges are never easy. By their very nature, they tap our vulnerabilities, create feelings of anxiety and arouse fears of failure. As couples, the challenges we face either bring out the best or the worst in us. Challenges have the potential to frustrate us, anger us and make us feel helpless. Avoiding them in fear never has a positive outcome. Too often, one or both partners respond more to the feeling of being vulnerable rather than to the challenge before them. Often, one partner has to deal not only with a specific challenge, but also with his or her partner's neurotic or unhealthy reaction. Be aware:

a neurotic solution may seem to work temporarily, but in the long run there is a price to pay.

Allen's Story

Allen came to therapy with two major conflicts in his life. One involved a love relationship and the other the career he had chosen. At the time he initiated therapy, Allen was dating a woman, Dana, he loved very much. However, there was one major problem: She was Protestant and he was Jewish. At the outset, this was not a problem for him or Dana. It became a problem when he considered making a commitment to her.

When he began to think about proposing to Dana, concerns about his family came to the forefront. His parents were strict orthodox Jews and he presumed they wanted him to marry a Jewish woman. He never addressed this issue with them but thought it to be true. As he continued to date this woman he loved and continued to think about marrying her, he fell more and more into emotional turmoil.

After several therapy sessions, it became obvious that Allen was stuck in a self-effacing lifestyle pattern. Allen had a large circle of friends and anyone who knew Allen thought of him as one of the nicest people they ever met. He was always doing things for other people, even if it meant putting his own needs second. This characteristic of "niceness", however, served an underlying psychological need. In order to compensate for his own feelings of inferiority and ineptness, Allen consistently sought approval and acceptance from all the people with whom he had a relationship. When he was successful in achieving this goal, he felt better about himself and liked who he was. When the goal was not attained or seemed unattainable, a range of negative feelings regarding his self-image came to the surface. He was stuck in a neurotic solution that originated with his feelings of inferiority and led to the obsessive goal of seeking approval and acceptance from others. Since he had developed such strong characteristics for this lifestyle, he was successful more often than not.

However, Allen's neurotic track was "derailed" when he found himself in the dilemma of wanting to please Dana and also please his parents, whom he also loved and respected. Due to his rigid lifestyle needs, he was imprisoned in an emotional standstill. From his perspective, and perhaps correctly so, he could only please one while disappointing the other. Not realizing the psychological dynamics taking place within him, he fell into a deep depression without a clue as to what was causing this major mood change.

As often happens when a person's basic solution begins to lose its effectiveness, Allen took on another layer of defenses in an attempt to achieve his psychological goals. Over the months, he became severely obsessive-compulsive. Not having the courage to face his dilemma, he turned to another solution in order to protect his self-worth. Feeling as if he was losing hold of the situation and himself, he began attempting to do everything in a perfect way. He transferred the guilt he was experiencing about his girlfriend and parents to things that he could control. He became obsessed with cleanliness around his house, including the washing of all the food he ate. When he arrived for therapy, he walked around his car several times to make sure he had not hit another car.

As Allen learned the philosophy and how people develop solutions to feelings of inferiority with the hope of nullifying them in some way, he began to see his situation from an entirely different perspective. He discovered that his need to please others had paralyzed him. In this particular situation, there was no way to accomplish his neurotic goal and please both his parents and girlfriend at the same time. Thus he went into a deep depression and chose the obsessive-compulsive syndrome as a solution. Without being able to turn to his basic solution to life, all his vulnerabilities came to the surface and were tormenting him with fear. His childhood feeling of inferiority and lack of love for himself were pushing him further into a dark depression.

These emotional consequences began to make sense to him once he recognized the trap he had set for himself. As he saw the pattern of his lifestyle solution develop through high school, college and then graduate school, he came to see his behavior from another perspective and the purpose it was serving. Unknowingly, he had been using this neurotic solution for most of his life. This particular crisis brought it to light.

In terms of his career as a general surgeon, Allen faced a similar consequence. He had chosen this particular career primarily in order to please his father and gain further acknowledgement from others. Eventually, the solution became the problem. Because he chose his career mainly based on his unhealthy solution to please others, he eventually had to face the consequences of his choice. As he was soon to discover, he not only hated being a surgeon, but also could not stand the sight of blood. The same scenario often happens in a person's choice of a mate. If a person makes the choice primarily with an unhealthy solution, the person might very well have to deal with the consequences of that choice. Just as Allen grew to hate his career choice, many couples begin to despise their marital situations and each other as well.

In both situations, his career and relationship, Allen had major decisions to make in order to rectify the consequences of using the self-effacing solution. This is always the case for anyone who previously relied on an unhealthy solution in making decisions and choices. There are always consequences that come to the surface. After much discussion, he chose to break off the relationship with Dana. Regarding his career, he moved to another line of medicine and ceased being a surgeon.

One could debate the worthiness of his final decisions, but at the time they were the only ones he felt capable of making. The main point, however, is the recognition of how we are capable of making crucial decisions under the dictates of our neurotic solutions. There is no quick fix to the consequences that are created as a result of living in a neurotic solution. Through therapy and a great deal of introspection, the hope is that each client learns the concepts of the philosophy and chooses to avoid the temptations of the neurotic solution.

Guidelines for Healthy Choices

Our healthy and unhealthy solutions have diverse underlying goals. The purpose of each solution and the reasons for making a specific choice in response to a problem are dictated by one set of ideals within the healthy solution and another set within the unhealthy solution. The healthy path operates under a different rationale and purpose than the unhealthy one.

The healthy track is permeated by a good sense of self, even a love of self. The person who loves himself has the courage to use his strengths and gifts, while at the same time accepting limitations and lack of ability for certain areas of life. He realizes he cannot be all things to all people, nor does he need to, in order to accept himself for who he is. The person of self-love is one who recognizes the reality of being human and therefore can be imperfect. He accepts feelings of inferiority but does not let these feelings dictate his responses to challenges or problems.

In contrast, the unhealthy person is ashamed of some aspect of herself and constantly represses any vulnerabilities or limitations in an attempt to feel better about who she is. As she focuses on this process of denial, she attempts to replace her real self with a false sense of self and gear all behavior toward reaching this ideal. This idealistic view of herself serves the purpose of excluding all limitations or vulnerabilities. The false image is created with the hope that no one will challenge or even see her limitations. Unlike the healthy choice, this unhealthy purpose allows human limitation to dictate choices and define who the person must try to be.

A healthy person is one who has empathy and genuine interest in the welfare of others. Applying this concept to a marital relationship, Alfred Adler explains that in order to have a full and cooperating partnership "each partner must be more interested in the other than in himself."[22] The marital relationship is perhaps the most significant place for this human quality. Having genuine interest and care for the welfare of our partners is a mandatory component for having successful marriages.

The unhealthy person puts the self first. Because this person is so obsessed with possible vulnerabilities and the fear of failure, there is little time to be concerned for others. When considering the importance of having social interest, the healthy track is so much more logical when it comes to enhancing and developing oneself. If we really care about another person and show this concern in an active way, we cannot help but develop our own abilities and enhance our strengths. By wanting to do our very best for another without the fear of worrying about our limitations, we are able to freely exercise our true selves and stretch our limits.

A healthy person has the courage to fail. Failure is always a possibility as we respond to various challenges. The person choosing the healthy track is aware of this possibility, but it does not dictate the manner in which he or she responds to a challenge.

Those choosing the unhealthy path spend time obsessing about failure's possibility. By choosing a neurotic track, the individual spends the majority of time attempting to avoid all failure rather than emphasizing creative possibilities. In part 2 we will see how all three of these guidelines—self-love, empathy and the courage to fail—affect the marital choice and the life of the marriage itself.

Ken and Julie's Story

Ken was in his late forties when he came with his wife, Julie, for marriage counseling. They had been married for over twenty years and, while they had experienced various degrees of marital problems over the years, an ultimate crisis brought them to therapy. Julie had discovered that Ken was having an affair with a woman half his age. Even with this devastating discovery, however, both were willing to see if the marriage could be saved.

Ken was a workaholic. He dedicated his entire life to a major insurance company in the city by working fourteen-hour days five or six days a week. There was no doubt that Ken knew the insurance business. He knew how to make or break deals and brought a great deal of success to his company. Over the years, he personally grew and developed into a top corporate chief, becoming very successful. Sadly, however, this was the one and only area in which Ken did grow. He did not know very much about himself as a person outside the demands of work, had neither much knowledge nor insight regarding the dynamics of a love relationship and seemed to care little for his role as a father.

In addition to his work requiring extensive travel, Ken also developed an alcohol problem and, unbeknownst to his wife, had numerous affairs. Partaking in the rewards of money and fortune, neither Ken nor Julie addressed what this lifestyle was doing to their marriage. Ken did not have much time to be a husband or father.

In terms of Ken's potential for development, he had the mind of a young child and he never gave himself the opportunity to develop characteristics or values necessary for adult challenges. He did not seem to care about the meaning and purpose of his marriage. All these things made the process of therapy very difficult.

Ken made mild attempts to resolve his marital issues, but it would have taken years of therapy and education to achieve this. Ken did not have the patience for the process and was unwilling to give up all the perks and benefits derived from his career. Perhaps as easily as he got married, Ken ended his marriage with the simple resolve, "Maybe I am just not the marrying type." Truly, he was not.

Relatives and friends of Julie and Ken were surprised when their pending divorce became public knowledge. From the outside, they presented the image of the perfect couple. To most, they seemed happy and to be enjoying a good life together. Little did anyone know, Ken and Julie were each actually doing his or her own thing for most of the relationship. Image might have its place and it certainly can fool a lot of people, but the reality eventually emerges, especially when the image is based on fiction.

The Importance of Perception

In order to better understand and apply the philosophy we're discussing, the concepts of perception and purpose must be considered and given a great deal of attention. An essential component of problem solving entails each person recognizing his or her own and his or her partner's way of viewing things and how these viewpoints affect decision making. At the same time, understanding the underlying purpose behind each person's behavior or response to a situation is also crucial in keeping conflicts to a minimum.

Perception influences two primary time periods in our lives. The first takes place during our developmental years when we are in the process of searching for a solution to our fears and vulnerabilities. The solution we eventually choose is greatly influenced by the perception we have of ourselves at the time, along with the perception we have of the environment around us. Over time, we slowly but steadily formulate a sense of who we are as individuals, especially in terms of what we perceive to be our strengths and limitations. These self-perceptions directly influence the type of solution—expansive or self-effacing—that we eventually choose. Based on the perception we have of ourselves, one particular solution is seen as more comfortable to us over another.

In addition to self-perception, the manner in which we view the world around us contributes to the decisions we make about choosing particular solutions. The people in our early years—parents, siblings, teachers and friends—along with various life experiences are all part of formulating this perception. M. Scott Peck reminds us that when "we are young, our dependency on those who raise us shapes our thinking and what we learn. And given our lengthy dependence, we are at risk of developing thinking patterns that may become ingrained."[23] With the equations in the following diagram, therefore, we can picture this dynamic of how our personal perceptions, once influenced by the environment, are now influenced by our personal solutions.

EXPANSIVE SOLUTION

I am above others in talent + The world is competitive
=
I shall try to win and dominate in every situation

SELF-EFFACING SOLUTION

I have too many faults + The world is very competitive
=
I should avoid all competition and conflict

In these formulas, by combining our perceptions we develop a modus operandi: a manner of responding to the numerous tasks of life. Both of these perceptions—of ourselves and of our environments—dictate the type of solutions we choose. At the same time, our perceptions influence the personality characteristics we emphasize and develop in formulating our personal solutions. We develop characteristics that aid and fit the chosen solution.

Sometimes while I'm seeing a couple for marriage counseling, I ask a question not typically brought up in therapy or psychology books but that often reveals an interesting aspect of the person who answers: "Which animal do you admire most?" Julie, the woman who was overly dominated by her husband, chose a dog. When I asked her what characteristics she liked most about the dog, Julie answered, "I like the fact that everyone loves a dog. It does not really have to do anything to be loved. It is always fed and it can sleep all day if it wants to. Also, it has a master to take care of it."

Then I asked Julie what her second favorite animal was and why. Julie replied, "I think I would pick the tiger. It is strong and independent. It does not rely on anyone. It rules over people."

I explained to Julie that the first animal hypothetically represents how she sees herself and the second animal symbolizes how she wants to perceive her spouse. Julie felt uncomfortable about her answers and what they indicated, but after reflecting a short while she could see the connotations as being the truth. She might have gotten more than she bargained for in her quest for a strong husband, but she was nonetheless seeking someone of this nature.

In marital situations, it is important that each person takes time to study the solution equations and perhaps reflect on the same questions I asked Julie. Then partners must listen to each other's responses. Each partner needs to apply specific aspects from his or her life to both parts of his or her solution equation as he or she sees it operating in his or her own life. This is not a one-time task but needs to be done on an ongoing basis throughout the years of the marriage. For a marriage to be successful in problem solving there is a need for constant reexamination of self-perception, for it is likely each partner has distorted perceptions to one degree or another. With each perception—of self and the world—we are capable of having clear and correct perceptions or distorted and biased ones. The personality characteristics we choose are drawn from the perceptions we have of ourselves and serve the solutions we create.

Each partner must be willing to admit it is impossible to have a clear or exactly correct perception all the time. The key task for each partner is to be aware of both possibilities in the self and in the other partner, since both types of perceptions play a major role in the decisions made. The awareness of self-perception is especially important in how we interact with our spouses and how we work together in addressing marital situations.

Cindy's Story

Cindy, a client of mine, discussed with me her experiences of going out to dinner with her husband and another couple. She explained she was usually very quiet and let her husband, Ted, do most of the talking. Cindy had presumed long before that Ted was the smart one and she had very little to offer in terms of conversation. Her equation might look something like this:

I am shallow and ill-informed + Others, especially my husband, are smarter

=

I'd better remain quiet and say very little

With this self-perception, we can assume that Cindy has played a minor role, if that, in the decision-making within the marriage. With this perception of herself, Cindy does not see or take the opportunity for personal growth. At the same time, she does not perceive or take the time to look for ways she can contribute to her husband Ted's life. It may take years of marriage for the relationship to become this extreme, but when it does it becomes a disaster. The husband, for his own psychological reasons, expects very little from his wife. It becomes a superficial relationship at best. Either of the partners, or both of them, might become dissatisfied with the marital relationship and the direction it has taken. Cindy's marital history is not unusual and even though it may take years to fall apart, so many often end with the parting of ways, leaving others to wonder *Why now?*

Perception takes on a totally different function once a person's primary solution has been formulated. Instead of perception influencing the making of the solution, it now becomes directly affected by the solution itself. After we have chosen our personal solutions, our perceptions become sensitized to our specific inferiorities and vulnerabilities we have emphasized since childhood. The more we feel and hold onto these inferiorities and allow them to dictate our lives, the more likely we are to interpret life events through them. This is especially true when we choose a neurotic path, because it demands us to be vigilant toward specific inferiorities. As the inferiorities are experienced, we begin striving toward our idealized goals.

Here is an analogy I use with clients to help explain how we are extremely sensitive to our fears and that due to our biased perceptions about these fears we have a tendency to distort reality. Imagine you are driving down a major highway. The highway represents the path or journey you take through life. As you go down the highway, you are very sensitive to the fact there might be major potholes up ahead that could ruin the drive. This is due to being aware and sensitive to the fact that you are physically, mentally and emotionally vulnerable as a human being. As you will remember, each person has his or her own specific fears as the result of dozens of childhood experiences.

From this analogy arises one basic question: Do you think the average person is more likely to emphasize the interesting ride, the beautiful landscape and the conversation or more likely to keep a keen eye out for possible potholes up ahead? Most people respond with the latter—that people have the tendency to be watching out for potholes that could very possibly harm them. The potholes, in this analogy, represent the fears, vulnerabilities and, at times, the terrors we have ingrained in our minds. Our perspectives on life events and our interpretations of these fears become key factors in our responses to these challenges that create vulnerability.

Jerralyn and Colin's Story

Jerralyn and Colin came to their first therapy session together. They were in their late forties, married twenty-two years and had no children. They both came across as very intelligent people who were finally about to address both their personal and marital issues. The crisis that frightened Colin was that Jerralyn was talking about suicide. Jerralyn confirmed Colin's worries but did so in a calm, if not passive, fashion. I asked Jerralyn to see me individually and she agreed. Colin also scheduled individual sessions, stating, "I'm doing this for her." He had little insight into how he also was psychologically enhancing Jerralyn's way of living.

It took four or five sessions to get Jerralyn comfortable with therapy. During the next two to three months she revealed a life of avoiding most social interactions while relying on her husband for a sense of security.

She admitted to "really not liking people" and often wanted to quit her job due to the lack of support from people with whom she was working. She explained that while attending high school and college she went through the motions more than actually feeling a sense of participation. She explained, "I always did the right thing, but I never had a strong feeling for what I was doing." Based on her level of intelligence and non-threatening personality, Jerralyn was capable of bringing her approach and attitude about life into her adult years.

Jerralyn had deep-seated feelings of inferiority and never gained a sense of purpose in her interactions with others. Because of her intelligence and hours of reflection in therapy, she came to realize she was completely wasting her life. During one of her therapy sessions when I referenced that life was like a journey down a roadway, she could easily see that she had left the roadway during the early years of her life and was living in what might be considered a "rest stop" of avoidance. It was a comfortable position for many years until she came to terms with the state of her marriage and the numerous consequences of avoidance.

Both Colin and Jerralyn were extremely likeable. It was hard to fathom that they both isolated themselves from life to the degree they did. Jerralyn spent her years in her self-created rest stop while Colin was obsessed with his career, working six days a week. Both of them, with their own formulas for avoiding vulnerability and all forms of anxiety, had created lives of isolation and disconnection. It was only due to Jerralyn's experiences of loneliness and discontent that this formula began to crack. She had all the personality characteristics to change her life. It would be a matter of how much courage and desire she had within her that would determine if she would make life a meaningful journey.

With oversensitivity to vulnerabilities and the need to avoid them, our perceptions tend to become highly sensitive to experiences that may cause us to feel inferior. Rather than seeing and interpreting people's actions and events clearly, we tend to distort them in exaggerated manners. It is as if we are overly alert and overly sensitive to anything that might even slightly reflect our greatest fears.

Consider this scenario: Two psychologists were at a convention.

The male psychologist stereotyped many females, especially if they were intelligent and aggressive, as being nasty and cold. The female psychologist, on the other hand, tended to stereotype males as only being interested in sex, especially if they showed any signs of flirtation.

One morning both psychologists were walking down the hall toward each other. When they got close, the man said, "Good morning." As he said this, the woman observed what she thought was a wink from the male psychologist. Thinking he was being crude, she said nothing and walked off in a huff. The male psychologist saw her immediately walk off without even saying hello and thought her to be rude. He concluded she was another nasty and cold woman.

If we backtrack and take another look at this brief interaction, we observe the man walking down the hall and saying, "Good morning." This time, without a biased perception, we are able to see that he had some sort of tic in his eye that could occur at any time. Because of the woman's bias, however, she put the eye movement through her subjective filter and reached a wrong conclusion. Then, not knowing what was happening from the woman's viewpoint, the man interpreted her turning away without saying anything through his biased filter and reached his distorted conclusion. The point of this brief and oversimplified example is to show how we can misinterpret many of life's daily events.

The following diagram indicates the potential to view another person's behavior or a life event through a biased filter. The biased filter is like a subjective magnifying glass that distorts or blows out of proportion the objective reality of what is taking place. It is when vulnerabilities are highly sensitive that people are likely to put things through this filter.

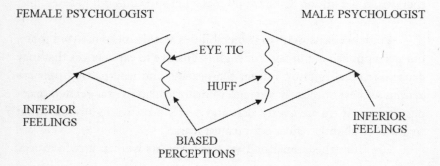

FEMALE PSYCHOLOGIST   MALE PSYCHOLOGIST

EYE TIC

HUFF

INFERIOR
FEELINGS

INFERIOR
FEELINGS

BIASED
PERCEPTIONS

In marriages, there are hundreds of brief interactions between husbands and wives. Given the importance of psychological biases, each partner needs to become aware of his or her own biases and the ways he or she is capable of misinterpreting interactions between him or herself and the other partner. Many arguments between spouses are the direct result of misinterpretation. Due to highly sensitive feelings, each partner may exaggerate cues or statements coming from the other partner and react to them according to this distorted viewpoint.

Doug's Story

Doug and his wife, Roberta, sought marital therapy after twenty-five years of marriage. During an individual session, it was discovered that Doug formulated a much distorted view of love during his childhood development. His father was hardly ever home and was, for the most part, nonexistent in Doug's life. To some degree, Doug thought the rejection, his father's choosing work over him, was his fault. He concluded that maybe he was not important or worthy enough to be considered by his father. His mother, on the other hand, related to him from a distance. Doug was born when his mother was older and years after his two sisters. He often overheard that he was a mistake, even though it was said in a joking manner. For reasons of her own, Doug's mother, older and tired of the motherhood task, held back her love and showed limited attention to her son. Doug came to the conclusion, still wanting to believe his parents loved him, that love was performed at a distance and felt intermittently.

Due to his relationship with his parents and numerous other reinforcing factors, Doug's self-worth was extremely low. He felt inferior and undeserving of genuine love. In a real sense, he did not expect much of it in his life. In order to counteract this self-perception, he developed a self-effacing solution where his sense of self was dependent on how well he pleased others and received their approval. Doug's early childhood experiences are exactly how all our formative experiences greatly affect perception and the development of a specific solution.

In his adult life, if people showed any form of disapproval, Doug felt insignificant and inferior. He put the behavior and comments of others through his biased filter (distorted perception) and automatically interpreted the incidents as due to his lack of being lovable. For the purpose of counteracting all possible feelings of inferiority, Doug developed the ideal goal to be loved and accepted in as many circumstances as he could in order to nullify his low opinion of himself.

In many of his daily interactions, Doug's biased perception was often part of his thinking and the conclusions he reached about situations in which he was involved. One can imagine how difficult it was for Roberta to deal with this sensitivity. As an adult, Doug's mood and behavior were often affected by his neurotic demand to be accepted and approved. Any significant person in his life—wife, children, boss, etc.—was given the power to define his self-worth. When any of them showed even the slightest disapproval of him, he reacted as if he was defeated and worthless. It became a vicious cycle. He always sought a level of self-worth by pleasing others. If achieved, he believed it was temporary and situational. When someone showed disapproval, he was resigned to the belief something was wrong with him. With this ingrained perception of himself and his manner of believing how love worked, Doug could not possibly have a healthy marital relationship. His distorted perception of love had to be corrected for the marriage to be successful.

No matter what challenges we are facing in our marriages, we should always ask ourselves a range of questions regarding our perceptions of ourselves and the world around us. Some of the questions we should ask ourselves include:

- How do I see myself in this situation?
- How do I feel about what is happening?
- What is my perspective about what is taking place?
- What do I think the other person's perspective is?

As we consider questions such as these, it is important to realize that our perceptions of ourselves and of the situation tremendously affect the way we respond to our spouses and how our spouses respond to us.

The Importance of Purpose

We have discussed how it is common for all of us to spend part of our lives attempting to avoid our fears and anxieties. The solutions we use are directly influenced by the perspectives we have on ourselves and the world in which we live.

Almost every action or response to a situation, therefore, has a purpose. The purpose can either serve the goals of the healthy track or the goals of the unhealthy track. When a person has chosen the expansive solution, the primary purpose is to attain power, praise and dominance. The person who has chosen the self-effacing solution has the primary purpose to be loved and accepted and to avoid rejection.

Understanding the concept of purpose is extremely important in all marriages. Most people tend to interpret behavior, their own and their spouses', on face value without considering the underlying purpose. This is especially true when the routine of daily life is upset with a challenge or when a specific problem needs to be addressed. When a challenge occurs, one or both spouses have the inherent possibility for being tapped by that challenge. Once they begin to experience their personal negative feelings, there is the strong possibility they will respond with their unhealthy and defensive solutions. When this happens, the real challenge or problem is not being addressed, only the personal needs of the individuals.

When a spouse responds inappropriately, there is a tendency for the partner to respond to the inappropriate behavior only, which further aggravates the situation. In turn, the spouse reacts to the other partner's response and then the other spouse responds and so on. Things can quickly get out of hand.

For marriages to function more smoothly and more lovingly, both partners need to keep in mind the importance of the concept of purpose. Every action and every sentence spoken has a purpose. It may be small or trite in some instances, but it nonetheless always has a purpose underlying it. When both spouses are on their healthy tracks, the behavior and the purpose are easy to accept. It is when one or both partners are tapped and respond with unhealthy solutions that problems and conflicts occur.

Given the fact that each partner can be highly sensitive to situations that tap his or her inferiority, it is mandatory that both partners be aware of the situations in which this might take place. To operate from this sensitive base, spouses should know each other's inferiorities and vulnerabilities. They should presume their senses of personal inferiority are going to be tapped from time to time and also realize how both partners have the potential to react in unhealthy manners when they are being tapped. When each spouse is aware of this possibility, the couple can dodge conflict by avoiding an automatic reaction to a situation and respond with more insight into how one or both partners are being tapped.

Rather than reacting automatically to the behavior or inappropriate words of a spouse, it is healthier and more beneficial to understand the purpose behind a spouse's reaction to a situation. Reacting to the mistaken behavior usually makes the situation the couple is facing more destructive to each of the partners. Primarily, it is destructive to the relationship. Keep in mind the dynamics underlying a healthy, loving and creative marriage: It is two people who know and understand each other's vulnerabilities. It is two people who know that a partner, because of feelings of inadequacy, will fall into a negative solution from time to time. A loving partner knows how to help a partner with vulnerabilities. A loving partner knows it is his or her responsibility to assist a partner back on the healthy track. Those who recognize this challenge and overcome it know why their marriages succeed. The couple having an unsuccessful relationship never learns this skill.

Jackie and Don's Story

Jackie and Don, both in their forties, initiated therapy after one of their many fights. They were in their eighteenth year of marriage and had had four children within the first seven years of marriage. In their first session, Jackie explained that she felt constantly put down by her husband. She revealed, "He always puts me down in everything I do. He always criticizes how I am raising the children." When asked to respond, Don explained, "I am just trying to be helpful. Maybe I bring up too many things, but I am trying to do what is best for the children. I think Jackie is oversensitive and I feel with her reactions to anything I say that, as the father, I am not supposed to say anything. Jackie is a good mother, but there are some things I notice and I should be able to say something."

During the next four or five sessions Jackie and Don continued making the same complaints and kept bringing up situations where Jackie felt continuously demeaned while Don felt he had the right to correct her when he felt something was done wrong. Both agreed to come to counseling individually in order to gain a better perspective on the situation. It was during these individual sessions both revealed a great deal in terms of their underlying reasons for marrying the person they did.

Jackie explained that she married Don when she was thirty years old. She admitted that she was getting panicky about her chances of getting married and especially having children. All her friends were married and parents. She met Don through a friend and the first few months of dating seemed to go well. During Jackie's third therapy session, she said she had realized something during the previous session. She explained:

> I do not know why I did not see this before, but I think I married Don to have children. It is not that I did not love him, but I know I really wanted to have children and I felt I was losing out on my chance to have them. We only dated for six months and decided to get married. I am really happy I have the children, but I am not sure if I love Don as a wife should. Ever since we had the children things seem to be getting worse. I am very unhappy and seem to be crying all the time. He treats me horribly and I cannot live like this any longer. I can see it is my fault for not getting to know Don better, but I am still glad I have the children.

Jackie was very honest about her primary reason for getting married. During the ensuing sessions she explained she could stay married to him if he stopped criticizing her all the time. She said, "Maybe then I could learn to love him."

Don, after a few sessions, was equally honest about how he was feeling. He stated:

> I was married once before and I felt really embarrassed about

the divorce. I started dating Jackie and began to feel better. I thought Jackie was beautiful and I felt good being around her. The feeling changed after a few years of marriage and the children were born. I no longer felt good around her. She had a much better job and was making more money than I was. I also came to feel that she only wanted to be with the children. I started to feel lousy about myself again. I hate the way I treat Jackie but only after the fact. These sessions made me realize that I put Jackie down so I can feel better about myself.

Jackie and Don married for many reasons, but the main purpose was revealed through conversations with them. Jackie realized she married for the wrong reasons. She also felt embarrassed and sad about their present situation. She had stayed in the marriage this long, because she did not want to face the reality about how she felt about Don. She thought it might work out or, as she explained, "Many of my friends' marriages were not that good, so I felt I was not much different."

Don's sense of self-worth had been extremely low for years and most likely long before his divorce. He explained that he felt very inferior around people, especially if they were successful. He was embarrassed to admit that he never felt deserving of Jackie and tried all he could to feel equal to her. He could see now the way he was going about it was horrible.

In the therapy sessions, Jackie and Don were challenged to make a decision about their marriage. Jackie and Don both realized they married with two completely different purposes. They saw the selfishness of each of their underlying solutions to their own fears and vulnerabilities. After a great deal of discussion, they decided to separate. During the separation, Don wanted to revive the marriage but once again for the wrong reasons. He explained, "I feel like a loser getting divorced for the second time. I know this has nothing to do with Jackie, but I wonder who will want me after this." During the separation Jackie admitted to feeling content. She felt horrible for Don's situation, but she did not think she wanted him back.

Summary of Philosophy

We learn to dislike our vulnerabilities not only because of our own attitudes about them, but also due to the reinforcing attitudes of those around us. As a result, we develop solutions in response to these vulnerabilities and spend a great deal of time living within our solutions as a form of protection from fears, anxieties and feelings of ineptness.

We should not be afraid of our neuroses, nor the neuroses of our partners. Neuroses are nothing more than human attempts to avoid negative feelings. We need to realize we are involved in neuroses to varying degrees and maybe even more than we may like to admit. It should not be viewed as a human flaw but something we fall into because of the very nature of our humanness.

By admitting to the destructive nature of our neurotic solutions, it gives us something for which to aim. Whenever we choose solutions that are meant as protection, we need to see how they limit the creative sides of our lives. It is of primary importance for us to admit that we can and do, at times, opt for neuroses. It is never a question such as, "Is my husband or wife a neurotic?" The more correct question is, "What is my partner's neurosis and when is he/she in it?" Hopefully, you realize the importance of asking the same thing about yourself. It is not a question as to whether you are neurotic but when. It is only in admitting and knowing this part of yourself that you can do anything about it. In marriage, this admission is mandatory. All failed marriages are due to one or both partners refusing to come to terms with their own humanness.

Tonya's Story

Tonya came for counseling in the middle of what she termed "another marital crisis." She was extremely angry and told me she had had it with her husband Josh. She shouted, "I want him out!" In an explosive tone she explained:

> He never seems to get it. Anytime I need something, especially when it comes to my emotional needs, he is never there for me. He is so blah about everything. I just cannot stand his lack of attention towards me any longer. I always feel lonely. I am better off without him.

When she was able to calm down, I encouraged her to give counseling some time in order to make sure she was making such a crucial decision for the right reasons. I explained to her, "You have been married for twenty-two years and have two children. It would be a shame to end your marriage without having all the pieces out in the open." Tonya agreed and we began to look into her personal vulnerabilities and how she was handling them.

Tonya's first recollection and recurring dream were revealing in terms of her personal vulnerability and feelings of inferiority. She described her first recollection: "I was driving to school with my mother. I realized my dress was torn. I told my mother and she began laughing. She always tried to make light of everything." Tonya's recurring dream was brief but telling: "I have had this dream many times. My parents fought a great deal. I dreamed of my mother packing to leave. She was leaving us all."

In the ensuing sessions with Tonya, we discussed her childhood history as it might have related to her years of marriage. When we discussed the issues she had with her husband and put them in the context of her emotional needs, a different picture of the relationship started to appear. With a great deal of courage, Tonya began to own her powerful feelings of inferiority and painful feelings of vulnerability. One could see that she never received attention from her mother and her mother often ignored Tonya's deepest feelings. Her mother's constant threats to leave the family convinced Tonya of how unimportant she was.

After a number of months of therapy, Tonya began to recognize how she was turning to her husband Josh as a solution to all her inferior feelings. Josh could help by responding in a better fashion, but the reality was that nothing would be good enough as long as Tonya was operating from her inferiority base. All the attention in the world from Josh would not satisfy her obsessive needs.

Tonya took hold of the psychological philosophy and began to see her behavior as a wife in a different light. Her husband joined her in counseling and both were able to see the mistake of bringing their unhealthy solutions into the marriage. Tonya and Josh needed to do work on how they related to each other, but now there was hope it would be done from a deeper perspective.

We have seen the need for each partner to have a philosophy of human behavior which emphasizes that human emotions created by our inferiorities often dictate what we choose to do and not to do. The success or failure of a marital relationship is dependent upon our responses to these human feelings. With awareness regarding the reason and purpose underlying all human behavior, we not only are able to problem solve, but also are in a position to help prevent many problems from occurring in the first place.

All challenges tap our feelings of inferiority and vulnerability. As we respond to these various challenges, including the challenge of marriage, our ingrained neurotic solutions are always a potential part of the response. When our neurotic solutions play only minor parts and we primarily react with our healthy tracks, we respond to the challenges with creativity and have a chance to be successful. If our neurotic tracks have major roles in our responses, then we are not actually responding to the challenge but more to protecting our vulnerabilities. This choice is always a temporary fix and therefore never works in the long term.

The challenge is to learn this philosophy and to understand it takes constant awareness to apply its components in a healthy way. The good part, after we have accepted all the concepts inherent in the philosophy, is to reach the realization that we have a choice. With each spouse working hard and helping each other to face the ongoing challenges, the marriage will be a success.

Part Two

Common Marital Mistakes

In part 1 we discussed the psychological dynamics underlying all our behavior and influencing all the choices we make. This philosophy emphasizes the importance of our thoughts and feelings as we face and respond to each of the challenges taking place within our marriages. For the majority of people, especially those who take their roles seriously, marriage and the raising of children is a daily and ongoing challenge. It is the type of challenge where people fail as much as they succeed.

The reason for this dilemma lies in the definitive omission of an overall philosophy of life. Due to a lack of understanding who we truly are and how we are affected by challenges, the risk of failure looms high with each task we undertake. When it comes to the challenge of marriage, therefore, it only makes sense that we stop looking at our partners and ourselves through superficial eyes. Through the use of a concrete philosophy, we are able to reach a greater depth of understanding and therefore tremendously increase the possibilities for a successful marriage.

Now let's apply the philosophy to the challenges inherent in all marriages. We'll also look at the underlying dynamics taking place between spouses on a daily basis. We'll focus especially on the primary mistakes couples make in their marriages and show how these mistakes lead to lives of tension and conflict. Be alert to the common pitfalls into which any marriage can fall.

The actual marital situations described will illustrate how we bring our solutions—healthy and unhealthy tracks—into the relationships with our partners. We will see how partners, at any given time, can either connect with their healthy solutions or their neurotic solutions. Recognizing the differences between the two and learning how to be especially aware of being "tapped" by our spouses will be an important task. Finally, emphasis will be placed on the mistake of allowing everyday problems to interfere with the relationships we are having with our partners.

As we apply this philosophy regarding the human factors influencing all our choices to the challenge of a marital relationship, keep in mind the letter V. Envision the issues we discuss as being on the top part of the V. The top of the V represents an incident or interaction taking place in a marriage at a given time. The bottom of the V represents experiencing all types of feelings regarding the particular incident or interaction. In these we are "tapped", feel vulnerable and experience a sense of inferiority and inadequacy. The key to a successful marriage is for each partner to be open and honest about experiencing these feelings and to see them as normal. Once we accept these vulnerable experiences, we can choose how to respond: either defensively or creatively.

Our attitudes and responses to these normal human feelings affect not only how we will respond to specific problems, but also how we will relate to our partners as we problem solve. When either partner refuses to accept his or her feelings of vulnerability, it is almost a guarantee that it will become an interference in the relationship. Any time a partner refuses to admit to the vulnerability taking place in a marital situation, it becomes a response that has nothing to do with solving the problem and everything to do with protecting the self from vulnerability. The denial of personal vulnerability is the primary factor underlying all marriages that are in conflict. It is also the major underlying reason marriages fail. Rather than helping each other respond to marital issues, denial leads one or both partners to spend time selfishly protecting their own senses of self.

We need to remind ourselves it takes time, patience and a great deal of practice to become good at making this philosophy part of everyday thinking as we begin to apply it to our own individual marriages. With time and practice, it can become second nature for each partner to be aware of and ready to admit when he or she is feeling threatened, overwhelmed, anxious or inferior. The next part is being aware of and ready to admit when he or she is responding to these feelings with a neurotic track.

As this new philosophical style becomes part of your life and thinking process, you will begin to see in each marital problem you have a choice of whether to be dictated by it or not. Remember, the activity requires openness and honesty. As we discuss various marital situations or you think of your own personal issues, do not be afraid to admit how you feel. Be especially open to your personal feelings of ineptness and vulnerability. It takes courage. The more open you are and the more you see the marital challenge for what it is, the more you will learn and the better chance you will have at creating a successful marriage.

Next let's look at specific areas I have found contribute to troublesome marriages. The lack of understanding with these issues is also a major reason for marriages failing. However, I also have found that as couples become aware of these common pitfalls, the issues can be turned into assets for making the marriage creative and successful. Some of these sections will overlap in terms of perspective and ideas. But, nonetheless, they should be considered separately as a possible deterrent to healthy marriages. Being aware of and applying the marital dynamics described is the primary difference between making a relationship successful or not.

Marriage: The Connecting of Solutions

To begin understanding the dynamics of our own marriages, it is imperative to consider an intimate relationship as the meshing and connecting of two individual solutions—a person's healthy and unhealthy tracks—with the two individual solutions of a partner—the partner's healthy and unhealthy tracks. When we choose marriage partners, we are actually connecting to both solutions available to us. Imagine your own personal *V* on its side and connecting to another *V* that is also on its side, as in the diagram. Try the visual approach. I take my left hand, which represents one partner and stick out my index and middle finger. Then I do the same with my right hand, which represents the other partner. I move both hands together connecting the middle fingers and the index fingers. The index finger connection represents the healthy meshing of lifestyles while the middle finger connection represents the unhealthy meshing.

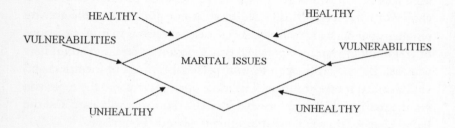

By virtue of these two connections, the marital relationship always has the inherent possibility either to function with the partner's healthy track or to function with the partner's unhealthy way of life.

In part 1 I described two of the most common lifestyle solutions. One was labeled the narcissistic and expansive type and the other the self-effacing and dependent type. In the majority of marriages, one partner is likely to be using the expansive solution, while the other partner favors the self-effacing solution. When choosing a marital partner, it is a rare situation where partners with the same solution marry each other.

No one solution is better or healthier than the other. They are simply different. The fact is the two different solutions that do attract one partner to the other can lead to a healthy and cooperative relationship or it can be a conflicting and destructive relationship. Presuming that likelihood of differences among partners, author Stephen Covey reminds us "when you put two people together in this most tender, sensitive and intimate relationship called marriage, if you don't take time to explore these differences and create a sense of shared vision, then these differences can drive them apart."[1]

Soon we'll discuss the one dictating variable for the success of the lifestyle connection, which is the degree to which each partner uses his or her particular solution. For now, however, it is important to note that there will be differences and that these differences demand mutual respect if the marriage is to be successful.

We are never perfectly healthy. Therefore, since it is impossible to do anything for perfectly healthy reasons, it can be said that none of us actually marries for perfectly healthy reasons. Throughout part 2, you will notice many references to this reality. All spouses have the potential to relate to each other from either the healthy track or the neurotic track.

Both the healthy and unhealthy solutions are part of and will always be part of a relationship throughout the marriage. All spouses are intimately connected by each of these lifestyle solutions. It is the responsibility of each person to be aware of how much the marital relationship is based on one track (healthy) versus how much involves the other track (unhealthy).

The underlying value to this recognition is that it gives each partner the conscious choice to make a decision as to which path to take. Awareness of one's own lifestyle tendencies and the awareness of a partner's tendencies move each partner away from ignorance into a conscious awareness regarding the makeup of the marital connection. A true indication of being unhealthy is when one partner rigidly uses his or her own lifestyle solution for the solving of all problems. Knowing where and when we are on our unhealthy tracks is a key variable to making marriages successful. Whether in counseling or reflecting on one's own, the most difficult task is the admission of being on the neurotic track. Without this admission by both partners, the marital relationship has little chance of working.

One major reason for marital conflicts is that most spouses do not realize they are connected to each other by both solutions. As a result, partners often unknowingly feed or support their own and their partners' neurotic solutions. Most couples prefer to see only the healthy connection. But when we are open to understanding our own imperfections—our potential to be unhealthy—then it only makes sense to realize we can connect to partners' neurotic as well healthy tracks. With more acceptance of humanness, each partner can readily admit when he or she is defending vulnerability rather than openly responding to the task at hand. Partners are also able to see when a partner has fallen into this trap as well.

In part 1, we saw how each lifestyle solution has its own particular qualities and characteristics. The characteristics of each solution can be used for either a healthy or unhealthy purpose. Each solution type, when neurotic, serves the purpose of having certain demands and goals be met. When a partner chooses an unhealthy solution, these personal demands or goals serve the purpose of counteracting any feelings of inferiority or fear. When either partner brings these psychological demands to the marital relationship, it is a sure sign problems will occur. The main point here is for each partner to be aware that the personality characteristics of each lifestyle solution can be used for a healthy purpose or used to fulfill neurotic demands. Both of these possibilities are inherently part of all marriages as partners face particular challenges and problems.

The narcissistic partner, for example, tends to value control and power. He or she is usually very competitive and makes winning of primary importance. This partner often comes across as confident, charming and outgoing. Caring and empathy are most likely secondary virtues, especially when these characteristics are being used on the neurotic track. A narcissist is usually a successful person, because of his or her emphasis on winning and being on top. When these characteristics are used in the healthy solution, they become a tremendous asset in a relationship. Without being overly emotional, the narcissistic type shows leadership and courage when making decisions and facing daily problems. When used in an unhealthy manner, the same characteristics only serve the defensive needs of the individual while the needs of the partner are ignored.

The self-effacing partner, on the other hand, values more the concepts of love and sensitivity. This partner is usually very supportive and considerate of the other partner's needs. Competition is not important to him or her, nor is the value of winning. When the self-effacing partner is on the healthy track, the characteristics of support and empathy become an asset to the relationship in problem solving. However, when they are used on the unhealthy track, the characteristics are used selfishly for the purpose of gaining approval and acceptance. While the narcissistic type can neurotically use control to avoid feelings of inferiority and vulnerability, the self-effacing person can use being nice and accommodating to gain approval and avoid the experience of feeling inferior.

As long as neither partner is rigid in his or her demands, the two can be cooperating partners by bringing their specific strengths to a particular situation. However, there will be times when one or both partners fall into their neurotic solutions. It is here where openness to this possibility is so important. In order to create the possibility for a successful marriage, each partner needs to admit to him or herself that he or she has an unhealthy solution and then relate to the other partner that he or she is aware of having a neurosis but may require help in recognizing the times he or she is living in it. Marriages are lacking and even doomed to fail when both partners refuse to be open to each other about their humanness.

When counseling engaged couples, I often see hesitation in accepting that we marry for both healthy and unhealthy reasons. Admitting to one's neurotic side is a difficult task and takes a great deal of courage. In individual therapy most clients are relieved to discover everyone has feelings of vulnerability and inferiority. They are also relieved and profit by the realization everyone has healthy and unhealthy responses to these human feelings. As they come to terms with their own vulnerabilities and the existence of their own neurotic solutions, they are able to face their problems more openly. With courage and honesty, they have the opportunity to respond to problems with common sense rather than being defensive about being vulnerable or fearful. Couples can make the same positive decision about their humanness.

After spouses present their issues in counseling, I explain to them the concepts of lifestyle we've analyzed in part 1 and I watch them listen to the fact everyone is vulnerable and has a neurosis. At first there is often defensiveness by both partners. Each wants to be the one who is right and prove the other wrong. Before we discuss their issues in depth, I encourage them to understand the philosophy. Once they can accept the realities of our humanness, I see relief. In addition, they perceive from the beginning that marital counseling will not be a one-sided affair and that both partners need to make changes for the marriage to be more successful.

In therapy, couples have the opportunity to learn their own specific vulnerabilities and how they are often tapped by a number of situations and, at times, by their partners. Through therapy they can learn the dynamics of how they respond to these feelings in both healthy and unhealthy manners. The knowledge they receive in therapy regarding how they connect psychologically to their partners often saves them from heated fights and conflicts. By understanding they have both healthy and unhealthy tracks, they have the ability to make a conscious choice and use their healthy solutions as problems occur.

Neither partner needs to be afraid to admit to the possibility of a marital neurosis. Understanding and insight regarding our humanness is the key to having a successful marriage. Each partner needs to put the so-called truthful cards on the table: "I can be wrong. You can be wrong. Let's help each other with it." A marriage requires full disclosure in order for it to be a productive relationship. Each person needs to have the courage to be honest about his or her limitations and fears, along with his or her specific type of neurosis. In doing so, partners will see how they can relate to each other with the more productive healthy solution.

Peter and Erica's Story

In marital therapy, Peter discovered he often took the role of big brother throughout most of his life. It was a characteristic he learned to take on in early childhood when he played the role of guardian and protector to his younger sisters. This personality characteristic is not necessarily negative, but it does have the potential to be if used for the wrong reasons. In his marriage, for example, if Peter used the characteristics of big brother to dominate or to control, then it would be destructive to the relationship with his wife. However, if he used this ability in situations where leadership and guidance were appropriate, then it could be an asset to the relationship.

Even though it might initially seem inappropriate or a demeaning way to describe an aspect of a marital relationship, we need to be open to the possibility there might be a time and place when being a big brother, with characteristics such as leader, comforter and supporter, could be very helpful. As with any personality trait that is part of the individual's solution, it depends on how and why it is being used. It is only when personality characteristics are used too rigidly, such as by the person who always needs to control and dominate, that it can be destructive.

Peter's wife, Erica, came to realize she was attracted to the big brother figure. In her childhood, she became accustomed to having an older brother who played the role of leader and also played, to some degree, the role of protector. The role Erica learned to play as a child and the type she was attracted to were not automatically unhealthy. The important factor in any marriage is not the specific role each partner plays or is accustomed to taking on but the manner and the degree with which it is acted upon. For marriages to be healthy, all role characteristics must be flexible. Each partner needs to be aware of the positive and negative ways that his or her particular characteristics can be used. A good marriage is when both partners complement each other's personality characteristics, but the partners must always remain flexible. The psychological purpose behind behavior, as discussed previously, dictates whether it is healthy or not.

There will be some situations when Peter needs to have the wisdom of his spouse. The same holds true for Erica. It can work both ways. A good marriage is one where both individual lifestyles complement each other and both partners realize there is a time and place for both solutions. In problem solving, partners will have their own individual perspectives on the situation and will have their particular characteristics and abilities with which to respond. When acting in cooperation with each other, together partners can make the decision as to which solution is the most appropriate in response to a particular problem.

Rigid Versus Flexible Solutions

To determine "to what degree" each person in the marriage takes on a certain lifestyle role and favors a particular solution in response to problems, it is helpful to envision an x-y graph.

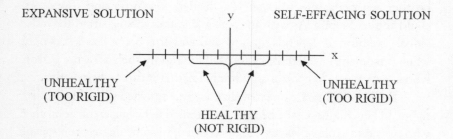

One partner is placed on the right side of the x-axis and the other partner is on the left side. Each side of the axis represents a different lifestyle solution. As we've discussed, opposite solutions attract each other and form a marital bond. Therefore, one side of the x-axis is the expansive solution and the other side is the self-effacing solution.

Given these two major solutions, the partner on one side tends to value the goal of control as a solution to feeling vulnerable and fearful (expansive). The partner on the other side is more interested in the goal of seeking approval and love in order to compensate for inferior feelings (self-effacing). In almost all marital situations, this type of marital matchup is likely to be the case.

Each partner in the marriage has his or her own psychological priorities (goals and needs) and therefore emphasizes different areas in problem solving as part of his or her solution to a specific problem. The differences in perspective and approach to problems become very obvious when a partner discusses a particular problem or when a partner relates how a specific problem affects him or her. Each partner will be tapped differently and will activate his or her preferred approach when a situation calls for a response.

In the graph, each partner's behavior can be analyzed in terms of the degree it is used and then placed on a specific spot on the x-axis. As we count away from the y-axis, it is our psychological task to discover where we would place ourselves on the x-axis. The farther out on the x-axis one is placed, the more rigidly and more often a person is using his or her particular solution. It is the task of each partner to evaluate the "degree" his or her particular solution is part of his or her life and the degree he or she uses it in problem solving. Once again, this takes honesty and perhaps a willingness to accept feedback from another. When this is accurately done, the partner then needs to make an assessment of where he or she feels the other partner is on the x-axis.

If the position we place ourselves on the graph is to the degree of one, two or three, then this is considered healthy. It means we are using our particular solutions part of the time but not the majority of the time. It indicates flexibility in problem solving rather than relying on one particular solution or approach all the time.

Being placed around the two or three degree range also means one partner is not too opposite the other partner's solution. By being closer to the partner's solution—either the expansive or self-effacing—the partner is in a better position to move across to the other solution when it is a more appropriate response to the problem being addressed.

We tend to favor one solution and that is okay. It is when we use it too obsessively as the primary or only solution to all challenges that we run into trouble. When we are positioned close to the y-axis, we have more flexibility regarding which solution to use. The farther out we go on the x-axis, the more time we spend in our rigid solution and use it no matter what the situation.

As discussed earlier, in marriage counseling situations, initially each partner tends to picture him or herself as the healthy one. In taking this righteous position, a partner depicts the other partner as being farther out on the axis and therefore rigid and neurotic. In order to reach a level of cooperation in counseling, all finger-pointing must be recognized as destructive. Marital problems are never one-sided. It may be the case that one person has more psychological issues, but it is never the case that one partner has none. To avoid these finger-pointing conclusions, each partner must first work to discover his or her own lifestyle tendencies and realize the degree he or she may be rigidly stuck to one solution.

Many times when a person is describing her partner as being too rigid and therefore the problem, she does not realize that she may also be describing her own rigidity. A wife, for example, may describe her husband as extremely selfish and say that he rarely considers her feelings or needs. She will often go on to give numerous examples. What she leaves unsaid is her role in the relationship and that her need for approval might very well exceed what is optimal.

A person who is rigidly set in one solution usually marries someone who is at least somewhat rigidly set in his or her solution. If this marital relationship has been going on for ten to fifteen years or even longer, what is it about the partner that kept him or her in this situation? The possibility is the accusing partner might be self-effacing to a point beyond what can be considered healthy. If this is the case, that person might not have the courage to stand alone and take control of his or her own life.

If one partner is on the left side of the axis to the degree of five (five is out of the range for the relationship to be considered healthy), the other is often to the same degree using the other solution. Yet some couples can last in this arrangement for years as long as each partner goes along with the other's emotional demands. We have all observed couples where one partner runs the show (narcissistic) and the other needs to be taken care of (self-effacing). However, even if the narcissist seems to function adequately, it can never be considered healthy. When a partner is rigidly set in one solution, a marital problem is waiting to happen.

Kevin, a client of mine, was reflecting in our session on the degree spouses can or cannot cooperate with each other's lifestyle solutions. He recalled a situation that occurred while out to dinner at a restaurant. It is a good example of a couple ingrained in opposite solutions. There were several couples at the table and the topic turned to golf. Bart, one of the men, looked around and addressed the other men: "You guys would love my golf club. They don't allow women within a hundred yards of the front gate."

Silence prevailed, each person wondering how to respond. It is one thing for a person to have this outdated perspective on women but even worse that someone would express it publicly. Kevin glanced over at Bart's wife, Gayle, after the statement was made. She was acting as if nothing was wrong. She seemed to be accepting her husband's outlook or was just resigned to it.

Using the x and y graph, one would say Bart was an eight on the left side of the x-axis. He showed narcissistic tendencies and revealed his sense of superiority, especially about women. He had no insight about how his statement would be taken by the others at the table, because he presumed he was correct and perhaps did not care what anyone else thought. The expansive is always about the *I*, especially in its extreme.

Gayle, his wife, on the other hand, was most likely an eight on the opposite side of the axis. By passively accepting Bart's perspective on women, Gayle revealed a self-effacing attitude about herself. She did not expect to be respected and therefore was accepting of her husband's humiliating statement.

Both their positions were far from being healthy lifestyles. However, as neurotic as their marital connection was, their relationship would most likely continue as long as both of them kept their rigid and neurotic solutions, the husband thinking he was superior and the wife remaining resigned to her inferior role. If, however, either of them decided to adopt a healthier outlook, it would put a great deal of pressure on the relationship. This might take years to occur, as we have witnessed in late-term divorces where one partner finally makes the decision to leave the neurotic environment of the marriage.

It is important to note we all have the potential to move farther out on the x-axis and slip into our neurotic solutions from time to time. Having this realization and the willingness to admit it is extremely helpful in creating a successful marriage. In the previous marital scenario, try to imagine how free and open a marriage might be if one partner admitted to the other when he felt vulnerable while also admitting he hoped to be superior and in control as a way of compensation. Imagine if the other partner also admitted to various feelings of inferiority and verbalized she put herself in an inferior position in order to hide from vulnerability.

When partners are open and honest with each other, they are able to achieve two major goals of a marital relationship. First, they do not have to be defensive with each other about personal vulnerabilities. Second, they can help each other resolve issues using each of their healthy tracks.

Agatha's Story

Agatha initially came to counseling for an anxiety issue, but she quickly turned to the subject of her relationship with her husband, Steve. She was seventy years old and came to therapy due to feeling overwhelmed by decisions she had to make. Her husband of fifty years had died during the past year and, along with missing him, she felt lost and confused. When she talked about her marital relationship, it was evident she had been extremely dependent upon her husband. He made every decision that came along in the marriage and was always dominant. During her years of marriage, she considered her relationship with Steve to be a good one, even though she was withdrawn and inactive when it came to making marital and family decisions.

From a psychological point of view, this type of marriage is considered unhealthy, primarily because both spouses were on the extreme ends of the x-axis. The husband had control over almost every situation. The marriage was more akin to a father-daughter relationship than a partnership between husband and wife. However, since both remained set in their ways, the marriage was able to survive. Agatha only became aware of her mistaken lifestyle solution—extreme dependency—when she lost her partner and was forced to face life's challenges.

In most marriages, the rigid solution is not consistent. Many run into trouble as the result of one partner changing his or her position on the x-axis. In doing so, that partner is also changing the way he or she responds to problems and, more importantly, the manner in which he or she relates to his or her partner. One way to envision this change is to imagine some actors in a play where one actor alters his role in terms of how he acts and what he says. This would affect the relationship with all the other actors. In real life such a change may be a move toward becoming a healthier individual, but unless the partner changes also, the marriage becomes one of ongoing conflicts.

Agatha, who was facing life without her husband, needed to adjust to a new style of decision making. Imagine what would have occurred in her marital relationship if she had decided she wanted to have more say in family decisions and also wanted her opinions respected. It would certainly have been a sign of personal growth for her if she had done so. However, it would likely have caused a major change in the way she and Steve interacted with each other. If Steve had been flexible enough to accept the change, then the marriage might actually have gotten healthier. If he was too rigidly set in his solution of control then the marriage would most likely have become conflicted and filled with tension. If it remained so for years, Agatha might have decided, for her own mental health, that it was a relationship with which she could no longer live.

What Attracts Us to Another

Love, I believe, is a necessary element in all marriages. However, the psychological connection—how the partners' lifestyle solutions mesh—is equally as important. A major component of an individual's attraction to another is how that individual's solution complements the other person's. In all marital unions, each partner's lifestyle solution—both the healthy and unhealthy tracks—seeks to be complemented and reinforced by the other partner's solution. Because many couples are unaware of having lifestyle needs and goals, most go through this process unconsciously. There are even some couples where love is not the primary reason for the decision to marry or for the connection in the relationship. In some cases, it might even be more of a connection of complementary neurotic solutions. Very few marriages succeed when the main connection is to each partner's neurotic track.

When an individual achieves a match with another, there is a feeling of contentment and even elation. We need, however, to be careful of these so-called positive feelings. When this match takes place on both partners' healthy tracks, it involves mutual respect and cooperation. However, when the match leans more to unhealthy solutions, the heightened feelings one or both partners experience are often misinterpreted as love.

Caution, therefore, must always be used as to whether partners are attracted to each other's healthy or unhealthy solutions. For example, one partner may require admiration and seek to be adored as a means of avoiding his feelings of inferiority. When this is the case, he or she is more likely to be attracted to a partner who has little interest in being the center of attention and little need for control. Such a partner is noncompetitive and therefore will most likely seek to avoid situations involving conflict. This type of partner will most likely overly admire the so-called strength portrayed by a controlling person and prefer to live in the partner's shadow. When this person finds a partner who protects the person from dealing with problems, he or she feels comfortable and relieved. This person might also make the mistake of calling the attraction love.

In all marital situations, the attraction and connection occurs from both our negative and positive tracks. When the attraction primarily originates from the person's healthy solution it simply means the partner is not using the relationship to counteract feelings of vulnerability. Partners who choose to live within their healthy tracks have come to terms with their fears and vulnerabilities and do not look to their partners to resolve or compensate for them. They are looking more for partners who can join them in creatively building a life together. In so doing, they are seeking partners who are also on their healthy tracks.

The opposite is true for those who connect more with their unhealthy solutions. In such partnerships, one or both partners are still allowing themselves to be governed by feelings of inferiority and vulnerability. In such situations, an individual will seek a partner who will fulfill the demands and needs of his particular lifestyle solution. In marriage counseling, these unhealthy connections become a main focus. To have a cooperating and loving relationship, both partners must be operating from their healthy tracks the majority of the time.

The challenge for anyone considering a marriage or for those already married is to figure out his or her healthy and unhealthy reasons for choosing a partner. In order to do this appropriately, each person must fight the fear of facing his or her own unhealthy needs. The unhealthy needs are part of the neurotic track and serve only one purpose: to avoid all vulnerability. It is not easy to admit to possible unhealthy connections with a partner, but pretending they do not exist does not make them disappear. In fact, ignoring them only gives them more power to destroy the marriage.

In individual therapy, the first and primary goal for the client is to become aware of her fears and vulnerabilities. The second goal is to identify her established neurotic solution used in response to her fears and realize the destructive nature of this solution. The same therapeutic steps are mandatory in marital therapy. The difference is that we must now consider it from the perspective of two people. Marriage counseling involves two people discovering their primary fears and defining their neurotic solutions to these fears. Then it is the task of both partners to recognize the connection they have to each other and to what degree it involves their neurotic solutions. Realizing the existence of both healthy and unhealthy connections allows people to be aware of the dual solutions involved in the relationships with their spouses.

Both partners, as they come to terms with their own and their partner's lifestyle solutions, should always be aware that one partner's lifestyle or particular solution is not better or worse than the other partner's. Each solution has something to offer. When it is flexible, there will always be a time and place for one partner's solution to make a contribution. When flexibility in problem solving becomes the foundation of the relationship, the marriage becomes one of cooperation and a happier place to be.

Since one solution is no better than the other, it can be said that each solution has certain qualities and traits that are beneficial to the partner. When these qualities are used for a healthy purpose, they act as complementary and supportive traits in a marriage. In the connecting of healthy solutions, each brings a unique perspective and ability to the challenges of marriage. One particular solution, at any given time, might be more suited to the solving of a particular problem than the other. When a different problem arises, the other solution might be more appropriate. The key to a good marriage is respecting each other's healthy solution and all it has to offer.

Todd and Cecile Ann's Story

Todd and Cecile Ann, married twenty-two years, are one couple who lived within rigid and demanding solutions. The two came to therapy very disappointed in their relationship. They complained their relationship had become dull and emotionless. Both agreed they were often sad and even depressed. They had been living this way for quite some time, resigned to the state of their marriage. Leaving the problem unattended for years led to further disappointment and increased depression for both partners. In desperation, they followed the advice of a friend and came for counseling.

In order to get a better understanding of why this couple fell into this emotional pit, each partner's psychological lifestyle had to be defined. Todd was obsessive-compulsive and could not stand facing the gray areas of life. He had many strong qualities, but his fears often forced him to face life with as little emotion as possible. He sought to avoid conflicts whenever he could. Todd's attempts to live in an extremely safe and protective environment, however, often led to boredom and a lack of creativity. As one might imagine, the consequence of his individual lifestyle overlapped into his marriage. Because he had a rigid need for things to be black and white (the gray areas tapped his fears and insecurities), there was very little excitement in his life. His healthy track, on the other hand, was rarely in operation and received very little in terms of stimulation or nourishment.

Cecile Ann chose to live her life also in a very limited fashion but with a different solution from her husband's. As a child and young adult, she depended on her mother and father to pave the way for her. She looked to them to protect her from all the negatives in life, especially those things that made her feel uncomfortable and inadequate. As loving and caring as Cecile Ann was, she often took the position of a "see no evil, hear no evil" solution. She was easy to be around and was always agreeable and accepting. She certainly did not bring any stress or tension to any situation, since she wanted to avoid these experiences herself.

While Todd was busy trying to be perfect and to have everything perfect around him, he never considered that his personal solution included looking for a partner who never challenged his rigid goal. His chosen solution to his own inferiority required a person who had as much dislike for tension and conflict as he did. Even though his chosen mate responded to her fears and vulnerabilities with a different solution, she became a perfect match and partner to his psychological needs. As they approached the marital decision, they both—albeit unconsciously—sought a partner who would not bring a lot of gray areas into the marriage. They both looked for consistency and a promise their world would be predictable and safe.

Prior to coming for marriage counseling, Todd and Cecile Ann were unaware that the needs of their individual solutions—to have things in black and white and with no tension—were not only smothering their healthy personal goals, but also destroying all the positive and creative possibilities in their relationship. Because their conversations were so limited and they avoided areas that would create anxiety or tap their fears, the marriage became boring and meaningless. Connecting primarily to each other's unhealthy solutions, it was no wonder they came to therapy very disappointed in their marriage. Unaware of the psychological theory of lifestyle, they were supporting and complementing each other's neurosis on a daily basis.

The consequences of Todd's and Cecile Ann's neurotic solutions were even becoming too much for them to bear. Thankfully, these clients had enough of their healthy tracks for them to counteract their neurotic habits. This is not always the case in some marriages. Some marriages have very little to work with in terms of healthy paths. With openness and a great deal of work, Todd and Cecile Ann developed the courage to view the meaninglessness of their neurotic goals. In doing so, they could reconnect with each other in a more positive manner. Awareness made them realize they had another choice. They realized how they had to stop allowing their personal fears to dictate their lives. As they began to live with more courage and with more openness, their relationship took a dramatic turn for the better.

Good Match or Bad Match

We discussed marriage from the viewpoint of its being a lifestyle connection and how it is the goals and needs of each partner's solution that acts as an attraction to the other. Expanding on this notion, it is appropriate to be more specific about these lifestyle connections and come to terms with the fact couples can either be a good match or a bad match.

Couples come to counseling because something is wrong with how the partners are relating to each other. The disagreements between them have been mounting and, at times, are ending in shouting matches and name-calling. From the lifestyle perspective, conflicts in marriage always mean one or both partners are living within and using their unhealthy solutions for one reason or another. By favoring their unhealthy solutions, they have created, at least for the time being, a bad match. When the unhealthy track is severe or the partner is not willing to change, it becomes the variable that destroys the relationship. However, if the neurosis is not too severe and there is a willingness to change, bad matches can be turned into good matches.

Each partner in the relationship has the psychological choice of how he or she wants to live and how he or she wants to respond to problems. As each partner responds to the various ongoing challenges of life, the manner in which he or she chooses to respond is primarily dictated by the degree to which he or she allows vulnerable feelings and fears to influence his or her approach to problem solving.

Perhaps one of the most important choices a person makes in his or her life is the choice of a marital partner. As is true with all choices we make in life, the choosing of a marital partner is a direct result of the specific type of solution one is using and whether it is healthy or not. Unhealthy solutions always create poor matches, while healthy solutions always create the possibility for good and loving matches. All marital relationships, therefore, should be discussed from the perspective that we marry not only for love, but also because there is a lifestyle match.

Since the choice of using the neurotic solution is self-serving and is dictated by selfish needs and goals, it always skews the reasons and rationale for choosing a particular person to marry. The healthy choice, on the other hand, involves an entirely different agenda. It is not self-consumed nor is it filled with an excessive need to defend vulnerability. It emphasizes the positives within oneself and yearns to put them in action. It looks for a partner who is doing the same.

The main goal in marriage counseling is to have each partner in the marriage reach a high level of openness and honesty. The goal entails partners sharing not only where they are vulnerable, but also how they fall into their negative and neurotic ruts to protect their vulnerabilities. When such honesty is accomplished, it can lead to an array of positive consequences. Rather than spending the energy on covering up vulnerabilities, efforts can be made to help partners live on creative paths. Dishonesty with a partner and oneself always leads to problems. At the very least, it cheats the relationship. It takes a great deal of courage, but those who do communicate with openness gain the benefits of satisfying, mutually rewarding relationships.

When this level of communication is reached between couples, each of the partners is able to reach a level of trust with the other partner, especially when discussing issues that awaken personal fears and vulnerabilities. The potential for tension between them is replaced with a genuine concern for how the other feels. Healthy tracks are creative, optimistic in nature and full of hope and promise. The healthy track always shows genuine interest in the welfare of the other partner, including the partner's fears and feelings of inferiority. Everyone profits from this type of attention and concern.

Unfortunately, there are many situations where one or both partners, prior to marriage, live primarily in their unhealthy tracks. When one or both partners live in denial, the decision to marry is usually made from unhealthy lifestyle tracks.

Catherine and Tony's Story

Catherine and Tony came to therapy after twenty-two years of marriage. They initiated therapy after Catherine caught Tony conversing with several women via e-mail. Some of the e-mails were of an intimate nature and some were discussions about his problems with his wife. As inappropriate as this behavior was, it still must be seen in therapy as a symptom of a more significant underlying problem. After a few sessions together, we decided Tony and Catherine would attend individual sessions to get an assessment of their perspectives on the marriage along with an assessment of their individual lifestyle approaches.

In Catherine's first sessions, she described Tony as lazy and herself as a doer. At the time, she was a highly paid corporate executive, while Tony, dissatisfied with his career, had changed jobs several times. This in itself was causing marital tension. Catherine was not only growing tired of being the primary earner, but also becoming more and more dissatisfied with Tony's lack of maturity, as she put it.

Catherine did admit she was a control freak, but she felt she had to become that way at a young age since her brothers were needy and always in trouble. She explained, "I was the good child and not needy." Reflecting more on her childhood, Catherine said she was closer to her father, who gave her more freedom and independence. She often clashed with her mother, who was more controlling.

Catherine viewed her childhood as one where she was forced to become an adult at an early age. She explained the members of her family took on little in terms of responsibility. She expressed, "I feel I missed my childhood as I played the role of top dog in my family. Where my brothers needed a lot of attention, I learned to be self-sufficient."

Socially, Catherine said she often stayed by herself, seeing girls her age as immature and therefore not worth being around. She expressed confidently that during her college years she "felt superior to my peers and I knew I would achieve more than they would." She further explained she had a few friends in college, but with the ones she had, she basically played the role of parent. As she grew older, she had a few boyfriends but said she "was the independent type and did not want to take any crap from them."

Reflecting on the beginning of her relationship with Tony, Catherine said that they met at work and that "Tony worshipped the ground I walked on." From the beginning, Catherine felt he was more interested in having fun and was not serious enough about life's responsibilities, as she was. Catherine, by her own admission, was often attracted to people she felt were needy. Even though she felt powerful and superior around these people, she was also often dissatisfied and critical about how they lived. In a similar way to how she perceived her upbringing, Catherine felt she had no choice but to be independent and forceful. As she expressed, "If I didn't get the job done, no one would." With this perspective, Catherine often became the scolding mother to those to whom she related. Tony, through marriage, became one of those people.

Many of Catherine's complaints about her husband were valid. Tony, by his own admission, suffered from a deep sense of inferiority and, as he expressed, "never found a place where I was comfortable or felt I belonged." In an attempt to avoid such feelings of inadequacy, Tony took very few things seriously, especially the values Catherine emphasized. Tony kept putting himself in the wrong environment. This was true by his not only taking jobs that emphasized primarily the making of money, but also committing himself to a partner who emphasized the importance of success. Neither of these fit his perspective and approach to life.

Tony admitted he was still in the process of "finding himself", yet often avoided the concrete work necessary to accomplish this. He wished, however, that "Catherine would get off my back and stop treating me as if I were a child. Her superior attitude only makes me feel worse."

After a number of individual and couple sessions with Tony and Catherine, I felt that their relationship was immersed in a neurotic bind. Even though Catherine's complaints had a great deal of validity, she had not, thus far, understood that she chose this particular type for definitive psychological reasons. Catherine, following the characteristics of the expansive type, was accustomed to being in control and extremely independent. It was her intent, based on the fact she felt she had no other choice, to be the dominant figure in any relationship, whether it be a friendship or the relationship she had with her husband. Tony, on the other hand, had no desire for control and, based on his self-effacing lifestyle, looked for someone else to show him the way.

From the beginning of their marriage, therefore, Tony and Catherine were connected primarily to each other's unhealthy lifestyle tracks. In therapy, both were very honest about their own particular approaches to life, but neither of them saw how their particular lifestyles were eroding the relationship. Since both were on such opposite ends in terms of lifestyle approaches, it was unlikely that they would ever find enough in common to love and respect each other. If either of them understood the concepts of lifestyle prior to marriage, the marriage would most likely never have occurred. Realizing their major differences, they both made the decision to separate.

Tony and Catherine's story shows how the connecting of lifestyle solutions on the neurotic tracks leads to a poor matchup from the beginning. Both Tony and Catherine brought their neurotic tracks into the marriage. The lifestyle origins of many marriages, especially if on an unhealthy track, often become the primary reasons for failed relationships. One partner connecting his or her neurotic solution with the neurotic solution of another is not an unusual formulation. Living within and through their neurotic solutions, two people approach the choice of whom to marry with the primary need to fulfill their neurotic goals.

Many marriages start out with the wrong lifestyle solution. In some cases, there is not enough of the positive connection to turn them around. Many spouses, such as Tony and Catherine, are unwilling to move off their neurotic solutions in order to become healthier. As a result, if they stay together they will continue to be in conflict with each other throughout the marriage and eventually the relationship may end in divorce.

A healthy matchup is possible in an intimate relationship even when spouses' particular solutions are different. As long as each partner's solution complements the other's from a healthy track, their opposite perspectives and solutions can be used as a benefit when responding to challenges.

Teresa and Jeff's Story

Teresa and Jeff's daughter Caroline was going through a problem in grammar school. It was a common problem for this age group, but a challenge for the parents to resolve. For one neurotic reason or another, some girls in their daughter's class were viciously picking on a few other girls in the class, among them Caroline. Jealousy begins early and is sadly often carried into adult life. The nasty girls attracted a large group of followers who were afraid of them and had a need to be part of the group.

The leaders in the group began making Caroline's school days miserable by calling her demeaning and derogatory names. She was mocked and verbally threatened. As a result, Caroline often came home from school in tears.

Teresa and Jeff were upset about the bullying and they turned to the school officials for help. The administrators had become aware of the problem and expressed that the couple's daughter was a wonderful girl who deserved none of the abuse. However, the administrators had not yet done anything to confront the situation. Notice all the lifestyles in action.

One afternoon, after another horrible day at school, Caroline sat with her parents. She was crying and could hardly speak. Both parents were being tapped by the daughter's sadness but in different ways. Jeff was affected, because he felt he had very little control over the situation (his lifestyle need). Teresa, on the other hand, was identifying more with the fact her daughter was not being accepted by her peers (her lifestyle need).

In an attempt to gain some sense of control, Jeff analyzed the situation and began to map out a plan of response. In the meantime, Teresa held and consoled their daughter. Jeff started to outline a five-step plan for his daughter. Before he had the chance to go through the whole plan, Caroline turned to him and said, "Dad, could you just listen to how I feel?"

Jeff tended to be very cognitive, especially when he was being tapped. His daughter's predicament made him angry and, to some extent, he felt helpless. When he was tapped in any way, his immediate solution was to form a plan. In this case, however, the timing of his solution was inappropriate. It was not what his daughter needed at the moment. Teresa's lifestyle solution was exactly what their daughter needed. Her solution provided the warmth, caring and emotional sensitivity the daughter required. Later, perhaps, Jeff's solution would be of use. At the moment, however, his method of problem solving needed to take a backseat to what his wife had to offer.

Parents are often called upon to respond to the imperfections inherent in social situations. Many social situations are permeated with individual neuroses that turn into a group neurosis. Parents are left with the task of helping their children deal with these difficult situations.

In Teresa and Jeff's case, they had different approaches to life's problems. As I've indicated earlier, this is not a good or bad thing nor is one approach necessarily better than the other. Both partners and their solutions need to be recognized and valued if they are to act as a team. Each partner needs to respect the other's psychological solutions and know that each has something to offer. What was affirmed in this scenario was the fact one solution may be more appropriate than another at any given time. In a healthy and working relationship, the key, once again, is to respect and value each other's approach to problem solving. When this is accomplished, the combination of lifestyle solutions not only is considered a good match, but also is extremely productive and creative.

Choosing the Right Mate

Once we have defined the type of lifestyle a person has chosen as his or her primary solution to problem solving, we can predict or at least make a viable guess as to the type of environment in which that person will seek to function. This educated guess includes the lifestyle type a person will seek in a marital partner. This is especially true when a person's solution is primarily operating from a neurotic path, which is always rigid and repetitive. For example, the narcissist who is *I* oriented and seeks to control and dominate will certainly seek a partner who has no interest in power and may be afraid of it. On the other hand, a person stuck in the self-effacing solution who demeans his or her own abilities will seek someone who is willing to take control.

When involved with someone in therapy living a neurotic track, it is not that difficult to predict the future decisions this person will make as he or she responds to various options in life. The healthy track is not as predictable, because it is open-ended and creative. The neurotic track lacks this creativity since it is based on a fear of life. It focuses more on achieving and reaching chosen neurotic goals. Once these rigid goals are identified, behaviors and choices become predictable in the sense that they must always serve the purpose of achieving specific psychological goals that the person hopes will nullify fears and feelings of inferiority.

Therefore, the greater the degree a person is operating in his or her neurotic solution (recall the x-axis), the more success one will have in guessing the type of partner to which a person will be attracted and the type of lifestyle pattern a person will seek to marry. If a person operates more from the healthy track, where a solution is not extreme or rigid, then one can presume that person's spouse's lifestyle is just as likely to be flexible. In these cases, the predictability of what personality type a person will marry is not as clear.

Everyone, when considering a marital partner, searches for a psychological match. When the search takes place primarily from the unhealthy track, it eventually acts as one of the primary reasons for marital failures. It may take years of marriage for either partner's unhealthy solution to reach its full force, but once it does, the relationship takes a dramatic turn for the worse. It is a common mistake to presume automatically that most people primarily search for a partner to love and to be loved by. When a person is living with an unhealthy solution, love is not the main consideration and in many cases not a consideration at all.

Neurotic people call this connection *love* when in reality it is only a comfortable feeling they get when connecting with others who satisfy their fictional goals. The achievement of a positive feeling, even though achieved in an unhealthy way, is often mistakenly interpreted as love. The person who needs to be taken care of or is looking to be saved may feel a certain rush or high when a savior appears on the scene. A person who needs to be dominant or looks to be admired might feel in love when he or she meets a person who absolutely and unconditionally adores him or her. In both cases, it is not love these people are experiencing; just a temporary high attained when neurotic lifestyles are connected. In marital situations, a relationship primarily based on this type of connection eventually becomes a nightmare. As in the misuse of drugs, more and more is needed to achieve the necessary high.

Neurotic solutions are not static. As a person grows and develops, he either becomes healthier or he becomes unhealthier. When the unhealthy solution of one partner continues to grow in intensity, as it may after years of being married, the demands often become almost impossible to meet. It is at this point in the marriage when the fighting and clashes in the relationship become more frequent. One partner is angry his or her unhealthy goals (emotional demands) are not being met, while the other partner is increasingly frustrated by the ongoing complaints from the first partner about demands not being met.

A primary reason for failed marriages is the way they start. Many marriages are formed as part of the neurotic solution to one's life. In such situations, one or both partners are using their unhealthy solutions prior to marriage. Fear and vulnerability dictate their lives. When people remain stuck in their rigid solutions, every major decision is made for the purpose of avoiding as many inferiority feelings as possible. Living within and through this kind of solution, people approach the choice of a partner with the intent of fulfilling their neurotic needs.

These marriages start out with misapprehensions and conflicts. In some cases, there is not enough of a positive connection to turn the marriage around. Marriage counseling begins to establish how each partner connects with the other in both positive and negative ways. Therapy teaches and encourages the healthy connection while discouraging the negative match. When there are not enough positive possibilities or when one of the partners refuses to let go of his or her neurotic solution, the marriage has no way of being healthy.

Couples who are trying to rectify a bad situation must be aware the structure of marriage provides an arena for each person's solution, be it healthy or unhealthy. Marital relationships often repeat the environment where a spouse's solution originally worked for him or her in earlier years. How a spouse related to others in childhood is often repeated with a chosen partner. As explained previously, the solutions we develop are not done in a vacuum. Our original environments play a tremendous role in the perspectives we develop and the solutions we eventually formulate in response to these environments. Once we establish these solutions and leave our initial environments, we carry our solutions with us and seek environments that replicate what we know and are accustomed to. As I've earlier indicated, in too many situations, the marriage becomes an arena where one or both partners can function with their unhealthy solutions.

Phyllis's Story

Phyllis entered therapy complaining of panic anxiety. Toward the end of the first session, she introduced an additional problem: Her marriage had become unbearable. As we discussed her childhood, youth and prior experiences, it appeared Phyllis suffered from an extremely poor self-image. She was in constant fear of authority figures and consequently did everything to please them in fear of experiencing their wrath. A constant terror hung over Phyllis about the power she perceived these people had.

More specifically and more correctly, it was Phyllis who was giving them the power by allowing them to define who she was. Because of the critical and demeaning way she viewed herself as a result of her early childhood experiences, she had no idea of her own strengths and gave herself very little credit. As a result of this inferior self-perception, she rarely realized she had other choices in responding to life situations rather than following the leadership of others. She never looked to grow or improve herself in any way, which only increased and compounded her fragility and fears about life.

Functioning on an everyday basis with this self-perception, Phyllis sought to be taken care of and protected from situations that aroused fear. It was as if she presumed she could not swim and therefore needed a lifeguard twenty-four hours a day, seven days a week. She looked for someone to protect her and assume total control of her life. Any attempt at personal expansion scared her, including the areas of career, a social life and especially a sense of self. When it came time to choose a marital partner, all her lifestyle needs dictated her choice. Her wish for a specific type of mate—one who would take care of her—was achieved. Tragically, however, Phyllis got more than she bargained for. Her husband, Blake, was a dictator who made almost every decision, large and small, and gave Phyllis no freedom.

Most marital cases are not as extreme as Phyllis's. However, many do contain elements of this type of disastrous choice. In many situations, the neurotic track of one or both partners grows in intensity over the years of marriage. As this occurs, one partner becomes more demanding on the other spouse to fulfill his or her emotional goals. It might start out as a small crack, but it often grows into a major hazard to the relationship. The full breakdown of the marriage may occur twenty to thirty years into the relationship. In many marital situations, both partners ignore the unhealthy aspects of the interaction. On the surface, many marriages may appear to be functioning and getting along fairly well. Many couples may seemingly go about the business of raising their children, attending various events, behaving well in public and so on. However, when some relationships are examined in greater depth, one may find they are connected more on neurotic paths rather than healthy ones.

Rose Ann's Story

Rose Ann, a woman in her forties, was married for the second time. Her first husband left her for another woman, leaving her with two children and very little support. Rose Ann understandably felt desperate and insecure. Her divorce reinforced an already established self-perception that she had very little to offer. She always presumed she would be rejected and now she had the divorce as proof.

Due to her poor self-image and years of misguided thinking, Rose Ann came to the conclusion that her only purpose was sexual when it came to having a relationship. Her ingrained bias about men reinforced this thinking. She had very few personal goals and, at this point in her life, depended on her brothers and sisters for any joy in life.

Her second choice in marriage was based on her fears of having nowhere to go and no other options but to marry again. She felt she needed a man in her life who would give her a place to live and help her with the finances and the raising of her children from the first marriage. Even though she initially came to therapy due to ongoing depression and anxiety, she brought up her present marital relationship and described it as being empty. She was lonely and sad. Paul, her husband, came home from work, almost always ignored her and went down to their finished basement to watch television programs all night.

Rose Ann came to therapy thinking she just needed help with her depression and anxiety, which she did. However, she didn't see the connection between her depression and her marital choice. She had already tried medication, but it had no effect. Unfortunately, Rose Ann was not ready to admit that depression was the result of the way she responded to and handled her life, including the choice she made in her second marriage. The themes of therapy became too threatening and she once again turned to her husband for protection, this time from therapy. Rather than dealing with the therapy situation herself, Rose Ann had Paul call to cancel further appointments.

In truth, therapy had become a threat to both Rose Ann and Paul. For the marriage to become healthy, both had to give up their neurotic solutions. This client made the decision to live in depression rather than deal with the emptiness of her life and marriage. Coming to terms with her inferiority was too overwhelming and frightening. Her husband's narcissistic solution was allowed to continue. He could continue to ignore his wife and do only what pleased him. His lifestyle preferred a dependent woman who would never question his behavior.

Ralph's Story

Ralph initiated therapy and complained about his wife, Liz. He had a list of the ways he felt she was inadequate and not living up to her side of the marriage. As he went down his long and tedious list, it was obvious that Ralph felt seriously wronged by his wife's behavior and lack of respect for him. He complained that Liz did not help around the house enough, such as in doing yard work. He reacted if she did not stand up and give him a kiss when he came home from work. Ralph felt that she ate the wrong things and was not trying to keep healthy. His list went on and on.

As he continued with his complaints, it became a challenge in therapy to figure out why he had this long list in the first place and what was underlying his grievances. One of our primary tasks involved looking for the underlying common denominator to all his complaints.

After a number of sessions in which we discussed other aspects of his life, Ralph's general unhappiness was apparent. He felt lost in his career and, due to his lack of success, he had lost pride in himself. His ego had been diminished and he was angry more often than not. Until he was able to admit what was really bothering him—the underlying common denominator of self-dislike—the anger and disappointment with his own life had to go somewhere else. In this case, his own self-dissatisfaction was being transferred to Liz. A very unhappy person was making another person's life miserable.

Spouses are often unaware that their complaints about their spouses have their origins in some form of self-dissatisfaction. Either in denial or ignorance, they are convinced that what they are saying about their spouses is the entire problem. Not being familiar with the concepts and dynamics of lifestyle and how we are affected by feelings of inferiority, partners rarely look for the possibility that there might be underlying reasons for their feelings of unhappiness other than the behavior of their partners.

In this marital situation, Ralph's personal feelings of inferiority and ineptness were being tapped on a regular basis. He needed to have power over something or someone. His lifestyle solution to counteract these feelings was the personal mandate to be successful in his career and to always feel wanted and needed at home. His career had hit a plateau and he was no longer experiencing satisfaction at work. No longer having this arena added further pressure to the other areas of his life for his lifestyle demands to be met.

The usual things that brought Ralph satisfaction were no longer working. His lifestyle involved the requirement to feel needed and appreciated, some of which was to counter his feelings of inferiority. He was going through a period where his solution was not working. Without being consciously aware of what was taking place within him, he lost the psychological solution that he hoped would make him feel significant and important. As a result of failing at his lifestyle goal, he began to feel more inferior and more inadequate. Yet, due to major stubbornness, he remained unaware of how this disappointment was affecting his feelings about himself and others. As a result, his wife was paying the price for his unhappiness and discouragement.

Neurotic Solutions Are Repetitive

In order to assess whether spouses are connected more by their unhealthy solutions or more by their healthy ones, we need to look for the primary or common purpose underlying specific interactions between partners. When a couple comes to therapy, at least one partner has a long list of complaints about the manner in which the two are relating to each other. Underlying this list is a primary theme or issue that is much more important than all the items combined. As we've begun to see, permeating all marital interactions, be they problematic or not, are each person's lifestyle approach and the psychological solution he or she uses to resolve the issues.

Another way to discover the common denominator is through the use of a math analogy. Each event that one of the partners is complaining about could be labeled as the numerator in a fraction. In describing marital issues, it is as if the partner is saying 3/8, 5/8, 1/8, 7/8 and so on. The numerators are all different and represent each of the complaints. The denominator in each fraction is the same. The numerators are important and need to be addressed, but the real issue is the common denominator underlying each and every issue presented.

Inherent in the common denominator is each person's ingrained fears and vulnerabilities and the solution used in responding to them. The common denominator involves how these vulnerabilities are commonly tapped in each partner and how a repetitive defensive reaction is activated when they are tapped. Ralph, the client whose problems we've been focusing on, had ongoing complaints about his wife, Liz. There might have been instances where his complaints were valid, but his long list was really the numerators. Underlying his complaints was a man who was very unhappy about his own life and the direction it was going. Primarily due to the lack of success in his career, his sense of self was diminished, making him both depressed and angry. Until he admitted what was really bothering him—the underlying common denominator—the anger and disappointment in his life would be displaced elsewhere. In this case it was toward his wife.

As we've discussed, most spouses initiating therapy are not aware of the underlying dynamics taking place within their marital conflicts.

Most are ignorant of the primary reasons they experience tension and displeasure in the first place. It may take dozens and dozens of clashes (the numerators) before the common denominator is exposed or it loses its effectiveness. It is during these times that long-term marriages experience crises. Throughout the marriage, partners are often convinced that what they are saying about their spouses are the bottom lines to the problems. Again, in the case regarding the disgruntled husband pointing out all his wife's problems, he was not aware or ready to admit how inadequate he felt about himself as a whole. His career was bringing him little in terms of satisfaction. Friendships were almost nonexistent. His neurotic demands were not being met. As in many marital conflicts, Ralph's common denominator originated with his neurotic demands and became the basis for most of his marital problems.

For a marriage to have a better chance for success, each partner must be willing to discover the common denominator in his or her marital complaints. Marital conflicts usually involve at least one partner's neurotic solution and his or her mistaken approach to problem solving. In many situations it involves both partners being on their neurotic tracks to some degree. It is rather common that many of the interactions between partners can actually tap into each partner's fears and vulnerabilities.

The mistake, more often than not, is when either partner blames the other partner for how he or she is feeling. It is a mistake, as we have learned, because many of the feelings experienced by either partner are the result of the partner's own personal inferiorities and particular lifestyle needs not being met. Since a partner's neurotic solution is not protecting him or her from particular fears, the partner often turns to the other person in the relationship as the one to blame. Adler warns of this pitfall when he explains, "When people look upon love and marriage as a solution for a personal problem, this is really making these [love and marriage] into a mere patent medicine."[2] In other words, marriage is never a cure for neurosis.

What Adler is emphasizing here can be witnessed in the marital situation involving Ralph, the abusive husband who was constantly berating his wife, Liz. His pride was being hurt by not being successful in his career. He had lost the psychological solution he had hoped would make him feel significant and important. The failure awoke his feelings of inferiority and made him feel inadequate as a person. Since he was not facing this disappointment for what it was, Liz was paying the price for his loss of personal satisfaction. In order to feel better about himself, he sought constant admiration and obedience from his wife. Not realizing his demands were illogical and neurotic, he allowed himself to believe his unhappiness was due to Liz's behavior and her supposed lack of concern and respect for him. He did not realize that his common denominator was actually a lack of respect for himself and the failure of his unrealistic emotional demands.

Alicia and Scott's Story

Alicia was upset about her relationship with Scott, her future husband. Recently engaged, their commitment, rather than being one of joy, started to create problems that neither of them had ever experienced before. Scott stated they were having trouble understanding each other. He explained it seemed there was a significant problem with giving each other private time or time to do things other than being with each other. He sincerely was trying to cooperate with Alicia, but no matter what he did to please her, it never seemed enough.

Alicia, when discussing her issues, came across with more energy and anger. She complained they did not have enough common interests: "I feel I am forced to give in to his interests. He does not seem excited about what I want to do." She continued by explaining she felt Scott wanted to be with his own friends more than he wanted to be with her.

In response, Scott tried to explain most of his friends were still single and he sometimes joined them for golf or some other activity. As he was saying this, Alicia interrupted that she did not like when she was not invited or was not told beforehand when he was going out with his friends. She explained, "He chooses to be with them instead of me." Scott felt, by contrast, they were actually spending a great deal of time together and he described many of the things they did together. His list was rather long.

Scott and Alicia were stuck in an emotional rut. Without intervention, they would just go back and forth with each other in a "she did, he did" argument. They needed to step back and consider the concept of maintaining psychological lifestyles that involved having emotional needs to counter negative feelings they intrinsically carried within themselves. Their so-called numerators were just repetitions of the same theme. Alicia felt she was not getting enough attention. Scott, not understanding her complaints, admitted to having a full social calendar but felt it wrong to have to give up all the things he liked to do.

Both Alicia and Scott had valid points about their relationship. Yet they were not communicating when they explained what a relationship meant to each of them personally. During their therapy sessions, we fully discussed the concepts regarding healthy and unhealthy solutions and then the partners were asked to put their issues aside and to consider how each of the circumstances might be tapping something else in them. Alicia, after much introspection, revealed a fear of abandonment and a self-perception that included a feeling of being insignificant. She revealed this feeling had been with her as long as she could remember. Scott expressed the fear of being separated from those for whom he cared, especially his close friends. He explained, "The divorce of my parents devastated me. I do not think I have gotten over it."

Alicia and Scott suffered from similar fears. Alicia's vulnerability involved the fear of being unimportant. Scott, having experienced sudden abandonment by his parents, presumed he was worthless. Therefore, he felt the need to surround himself with many people to counteract these feelings. Where Alicia and Scott differed was in their solutions to these feelings of inferiority. Alicia fought for attention and saw each situation in her life as a threat to her fear of being insignificant. Every situation, especially one involving a love relationship, became an arena for her emotional needs (demands) to be satisfied. By using the goal of always staying in control, she made sure Scott always treated her as number one. Any diversion from this personal goal, such as Scott going out with friends, tapped into her negative feelings about herself.

Scott, in response to his childhood hurts, also tried to make sure he would never experience feelings of abandonment again. His solution was to keep distant from all people who mattered or certainly not to totally rely on them so as not to risk being hurt. His goal was to make sure he never allowed any one person to have the power to disappoint him again.

The challenge in therapy was to help Scott and Alicia realize everyone develops solutions to fears and vulnerabilities. Alicia was oversensitive to any form of rejection. Scott claimed innocence by being independent, while giving the image he was well-rounded. It was his defensive way of playing safe. The more Scott was distant, the more Alicia's sense of unimportance was tapped. She began choosing her defensive and neurotic solution by forcing Scott to always pay attention to her. Every time Scott went out with his friends, Alicia saw this as a threat to her significance. Every time Alicia demanded more, Scott saw it as a threat to his solution of keeping a distance.

Using the symbol of the *V* turned on its side, it can be seen that Scott and Alicia were connected by their neurotic solutions. They were misusing their love relationship as a means to overcome their own feelings of inferiority. It was if Alicia was saying, "I'll make sure that I am never insignificant by getting Scott to prove his love for me in every situation." Scott was saying via his neurotic solution, "I will never give myself fully to another person, since it allows for the possibility of being hurt."

If they were ever to get along as a couple, Alicia and Scott needed to address their fears and their neurotic solutions.

Couples who have not come to terms with their personal feelings of inferiority and who have not identified their unhealthy neurotic solutions to these feelings, no matter with whom they had an intimate relationship, most likely operate on their lifetime scenarios. These, to a degree which must be determined, are their reasons for choosing a particular partner. As with many others, not being aware of their neurotic demands, Scott and Alicia looked for the type of mate where their solutions could be played out. Alicia was in search of a mate who gave her more attention while Scott felt the need to not trust another person fully and therefore had to keep pushing others back from a full relationship. Alicia's behavior was suited to this defensive exercise. This occurs at times in all marriages, but in destructive relationships it happens more often.

The feeling of inferiority is present in all of us. In order to counteract it, especially among those who are primarily on their neurotic tracks, we pick partners whose behavior will allow us to activate our neurotic solutions. This is a reality in many marriages. We pick partners who fuel the perspectives we have on life and partners who antagonize the vulnerable feelings. As a result, we can keep using our neurotic solutions and feel justified in doing so.

Scott and Alicia did not see the common denominator of their complaints and arguments. Each was living off his or her neurotic solution a great deal but justifying it by complaining about the other's behavior. Both were allowing their personal feelings of fear and vulnerability to dictate their interpretations of events and therefore influence their behavior. If left unchanged, the partnership would become a vicious cycle as both tried to fulfill their neurotic demands. As we discussed earlier, marital problems are always individual problems first. The relationship problem is certainly important, but secondary. While living within their unhealthy lifestyles, Alicia would always seek out a Scott type and Scott would look for an Alicia type. Each would have his or her neurosis energized and refueled by the other. All marital relationships must look out for this possibility, for it leads to failure.

Realizing When Your Spouse "Taps" You

I have defined *being tapped*, which I consider an important concept, as a time when feelings of inferiority and vulnerability are awakened. The possibilities for being "tapped" in a marital relationship are endless. The challenge of marriage involves more situations and more variables than any other challenge we have. Along with many problematic situations that are inherent in a one-on-one relationship, there is also a tremendous amount of interplay between partners as they attempt to resolve the endless array of problems and challenges of a marital and family life. In order to increase the chances of having a successful marriage, couples need to reach a full recognition of this human condition. In long-term marriages, the lack of this dynamic is what can eventually wear down the relationship to where there is very little foundation left.

We must expect to have problems and challenges in each and every stage of our lives. For the institution of marriage, nothing could be truer. As spouses interrelate with each other, the vulnerability factor of each partner is often present. Everyone struggles with this human dilemma, but none more than the married couple. One partner can have his or her insecurities exposed with just a simple phrase from his or her partner. Or a specific action by one partner can set off personal feelings of vulnerability and inferiority in the other partner in a matter of seconds. We need to be reminded of the reality. Problems and challenges are a part of all aspects of life and they potentially make us vulnerable.

Typically, defense mechanisms are activated and used as a means to nullify the vulnerability being experienced. However, when a partner is open to having feelings of vulnerability or anxiety, there is less need for a defensive reaction. Even a small action, however minor, by a partner can set off a definitive uneasiness in the other partner.

Howard's Story

In one of our therapy sessions, Howard revealed how any one event can carry the potential for exposing vulnerability and even arousing anxiety and fear. When he was a child, Howard's father drank a great deal. As a direct result of the drinking, his father got violent headaches at night. Prior to going to bed, Howard's father put heating lotion on his forehead and temples with the hope of achieving some relief. When Howard was a child, the strong smell of heating lotion permeated the second floor of his house on a nightly basis. For him, the smell itself was connected to his father's tragic lifestyle and all the sadness it created in his family. At times, the sadness led to depression and even despair.

During the first few weeks of his marriage, Howard arrived home one evening to a strange, strong smell in the house. He quickly realized it was the smell of heating lotion. His senses were alerted and an intense mood overcame him. Howard was immediately aware of the connection between the tension he felt and the strong odor in the house.

Howard was not aware his wife had sprained her ankle that day. She put heating lotion on it for some relief and it just happened to be the same brand Howard's father had used. It was as if he was a young boy again walking up to the second floor of his childhood home. Fortunately, due to his recognition of the tie between the stimulus and its effect, Howard was immediately aware of what was happening to him. He understood the negative feelings he was experiencing. Rather than reacting negatively to what was taking place within him, he was able to share his emotional reaction with his wife and the reasons for the way he was feeling.

As small as this event may seem, it is an example of how even minor situations can tap us and hold the potential for affecting the marital relationship. If the client was not aware of having a terrible memory awakened, his reaction to the smell would have been much different. Without awareness, his negative emotions might have come out in an inappropriate manner and potentially been directed toward his wife.

The client's experience, although brief and minor, emphasizes the importance of understanding the key fears and vulnerabilities one has internalized since childhood. Repression sometimes works without consequence in many areas of life, but it is less likely to work as consistently in a marriage. There is so much involved in an intimate relationship. More than any other life situation, the percentages are high that many of the interactions between spouses will get through their defensive systems and then tap their personal vulnerabilities.

For a marriage to be successful, marital partners need to recognize that defensive systems, the denial of vulnerability, always act as interferences to having a working relationship. In order to best handle these vulnerabilities, each person in the marriage needs to learn the dynamics of how any one stimulus coming from a partner, verbal or otherwise, can awaken personal feelings of inferiority. Thomas Moore, reflecting on this dynamic, explains that being tapped by our partners "always points in the direction of both what the soul needs and what we are defending against."[3] When awareness of vulnerability is applied correctly, there will be times in the marriage when a person can easily see the connection between what a spouse is saying and a deep inferiority feeling the person internalized long ago. It is at this point where there is an opportunity to be defensive or to assist each other with the feelings of vulnerability.

By understanding the inner workings of all our lifestyles—inferiorities and the solutions created in response to them—we can be more aware of the manners in which internalized feelings are hidden behind our defensive walls. This is one of the most important steps to having a good marital relationship. Throughout a marriage, spouses are challenged to learn and re-learn how they are vulnerable and that these vulnerabilities can be easily affected. Admitting to and taking responsibility for one's own feelings when they are tapped is at the top of the list when it comes to having a marriage that works.

Craig's Story

In one therapy session, Craig related a recurring dream he had since childhood. It always involved running from something of which he was frightened. No matter how hard he tried, he could never run fast enough. Even as he tried to run faster, his legs never moved quickly enough. Throughout the dream, he was constantly fearful about getting caught. This repeating theme in his dreams indicated he often felt personally inadequate about his own abilities. As a result of his self-perception (being inadequate), he was especially sensitive to situations that challenged his strengths or could possibly expose his limitations.

Not being aware of the dynamics of lifestyle, Craig became irritable and a difficult husband to live with when his inferiority was tapped. Since he was overly sensitive to any form of criticism that might expose his feeling of inadequacy, his wife could never question him without risking his negative reaction. Even when it was obvious to his wife that a particular situation or criticism brought about some form of inadequacy feelings in Craig, he was still unable to admit to the real feeling when it occurred. In an attempt to avoid feelings of inadequacy, he often exploded in anger if his wife questioned him about his mood. Punching holes in walls was not unusual. Because he was so sensitive to being possibly inadequate, none of his behavior could be questioned, including when he drank too much or came home too late at night. His feelings of being inadequate and the need to defend against that feeling dictated his life.

Over time in the marriage, Craig began to see his wife as annoying to be around. The distance between them widened as the months and years went on. By the time the couple came to therapy decades into the marriage, there was a huge gap between them, physically and emotionally.

Craig found therapy very difficult. Especially in the sessions where his wife was present, Craig was overly sensitive to criticism and felt he was picked on unfairly when part of the session addressed him. Either he rejected the feedback about his behavior or he gave some lame excuse to explain himself. He could not listen to what was being discussed about his behavior, for he was reacting more to his fear of inadequacy. Throughout most of the conversations in therapy, he was often busy protecting his specific inferiority. Not wanting to reveal his feelings of inadequacy, Craig continued to avoid as many challenging questions as he could. If pressed or confronted by his wife, he reacted with anger and in some cases attacked her verbally in an attempt to demean her.

The challenge in therapy was to get Craig "relaxed" with the fact everyone feels inadequate and that there are better ways to deal with these feelings than with avoidance, denial or attacking another person. Craig needed to come to terms with the fact that all human beings, at one time or another, spend time trying to deny feelings of vulnerability. If Craig could accept this reality and apply it to himself, he would be in a position to recognize his own defensive system at work. For the marriage to be successful, this realization was mandatory.

Putting Too Much in the Marital Bucket

Marriage often acts as an extended environment for one's negative or neurotic solution to life. If this unhealthy solution is not corrected before or during the marriage, the unhealthy solution becomes a major deterrent to having a productive and creative relationship. In fact, by its very nature it creates a negative environment for all those involved. While accepting the importance of this factor, it is appropriate at this time to point out that there are possible mistakes made by spouses even when they are living within their healthy solutions.

The first of these mistakes seems to occur in most marriages at one time or another. I have observed in my years of being a marital counselor that many couples allow an endless array of outside burdens and problems to interfere with how the spouses relate to each other. By this I mean one or both partners mistakenly allow life's burdens to enter the marriage in such a way that the burdens often begin to erode the relationship itself. Rather than viewing each individual challenge for what it is—a challenge but not a marital contention—partners often allow such challenges to become part of their definition of the relationship. The relationship and the outside burdens become one and the same. The burdens begin to define the marriage.

All married couples must deal with numerous problems and challenges of life, such as financial problems, parenting and sickness. Since these challenges rarely occur one at a time, they have the potential to and often do become overwhelming burdens that begin to take a toll on each partner. As each partner continues to feel the continuous weight of the problems, the consequences of handling these burdens begin to cross over into the marital relationship itself. This is especially true when a specific problem lingers or seems irresolvable. One or both partners, feeling frustrated, incompetent and vulnerable, will then often turn to the other to solve the problems and expect the other to make them go away. Even worse, one may begin to blame the other partner for having these problems in the first place.

As the challenges increase both in number and intensity, the couple, perhaps without realizing it, places each and every one of these problems in what I refer to as the marital bucket. Over time, dictated by the number of issues with which a couple needs to deal, the bucket itself becomes heavier and more burdensome. As new problems arise, they too are thrown into the marital bucket. Before long, the bucket is overflowing. Over time, this mistaken process begins to pollute the marriage and, even more mistakenly, becomes synonymous with the marriage itself.

To correct this process that occurs in far too many marriages, couples need to first of all recognize this destructive practice. It is not the fault of the marriage that many of life's problems or challenges occur. Again, the thing to keep in mind is that partners must separate the challenges of life from the marriage itself. Money, for example, is often made into a contentious marital issue when it really should be considered one of a long list of life problems. When issues such as money are automatically put into the marital bucket, they become not only a money issue, but a marital problem as well.

Partners often bring into the marriage huge expectations as to what the marriage should be able to handle and what it should be able to resolve. Some couples even view marriage as a solution to all of life's problems, when in fact it is just part of life and only part of the solution. Thomas Moore reiterates this theme when he explains, "Like everything else in life, marriage is not unadulterated happiness—it is part of becoming a person."[4] And as part of becoming a more complete person, the institution of marriage was never meant to solve all the problems we face as couples nor be the solution to all individual problems. It is never meant to be a haven to protect one from personal and family difficulties. As in any area of life, we need to presume we will have problems and it is an ongoing challenge to learn ways to resolve them. If they cannot be resolved, especially immediately, we must learn ways to deal with life's imperfect aspects.

Even though this factor regarding problem solving may seem evident, many couples still make the mistake of making outside burdens and the relationship one and the same. Couples often come to therapy for marital counseling and it quickly becomes obvious that their situations are not necessarily relationship problems. It is marital only in the secondary sense. Their issues have more to do with how they are handling life's problems as a team and the effect these problems are having on each of the spouses as individuals.

As I've indicated before and will continue to stress, we need to remind ourselves on an ongoing basis that most problems are individual problems first and only marital as a consequence of the real issue. Problems will always tap our feelings of inadequacy and create vulnerability. When this caution is ignored, there is a tendency for one or both partners to blame the other for certain negative feelings they are having. To avoid this common transference, partners need to be honest about feelings that are inherent in them and how they are awakened by the daily problems and challenges of life. Everyone has feelings of inferiority and vulnerability and they were there long before marriage. Taking responsibility for our own inferiority feelings is the first step in not making them a marital issue. The second step is to be aware how our vulnerabilities are affected by our problems.

In all marriages—especially after the honeymoon stage is over—it quickly becomes apparent that neither partner can handle or resolve every single problem. Yet, even given this reality, there is still the tendency for each partner to use his or her unhealthy solution in problem solving. Frustration, disappointment and even anger quickly follow when the expectations are not met.

When this type of scenario takes place between couples, it is not a marital issue. It is more one or both partners being dishonest about their abilities, limitations and needs. It is one or both partners existing in their neurotic tracks and failing to see not only that the demands placed on their partners are ridiculous, but also their expectations for themselves are equally ridiculous.

When we ask an electrician to come to our home, we only expect him to fix the electric switch. When we call a plumber, we only ask him to fix the leak. The carpenter we employ needs only to fix the cabinet. However, when it comes to our spouses, we illogically expect them to be good at all things, not excluding to be perfect in love.

In order to avoid putting too many problems in the marital bucket, each partner should make a list of the things that tap him or her. The list should include issues or events that make him or her feel inadequate or inferior. Once this is done, it is important to share this information with the other partner. Imagine just sitting down with your spouse from time to time and simply saying to each other, "The things that make me feel inadequate, overwhelmed, anxious and fearful are…" After making this honest admission, then the partners need to pledge to each other they will not make it part of the marital relationship. They need to promise to deal with such issues together and not with blame. This process is the only way for spouses to know each other for who they are. It is the only way to give each other the support and love both need.

Ron and Susan's Story

In therapy, when Ron, married for twenty-five years, made a list of what tapped him, it was a long one. Ron grew up in a world of chaos. There was also a great deal of competition both within and outside his family. There were always various degrees of arguments and fighting. By the time he became a young adult, Ron could no longer stand the atmosphere of tension. It not only made him feel uncomfortable, but also at times made him terrified and overwhelmed with the dog-eat-dog environment. Even when there were times of peace, he still anxiously waited for the next confrontation to begin. Tension and conflict of any kind terrified him.

The psychological goal Ron had developed as a child, making sure he never ignited these fears of chaos, was to insist he have total peace in his environment. He brought this goal into his marriage and family life.

Prior to therapy, Ron did not realize how strong this need was. But even as we worked together and he became more aware and grew to know this expectation for total peace was one impossible to achieve, the temptation and desire for this goal was always there. There were, of course, many occasions in his marital home when his expectations were not met. It was during the less than peaceful times that Ron had his anxieties tapped, just as if he were back in his childhood. As a result of being tapped and not achieving his neurotic demand, he often became frustrated and reacted in anger. Members of his family then reacted to his anger, not realizing its origin. Not seeing it as an individual problem, he often presumed it had something to do with the marriage. When dealing with problems that actually did disturb the so-called peace, out came the marital bucket. He saw everything as being a marital issue rather than a personal issue.

Ron's wife, Susan, was also very sensitive to situations that felt overwhelming. Whether it was due to finances, the children or some other issue, she was often tapped when situations created insecurity. As a child, she also grew up under a great deal of tension, but her psychological solution differed from her husband's. In response to anxious feelings created by uncertainty, she sought the ideal of having total security. In the initial stages of the marriage, she, like Ron, did not see the problems as personal ones and therefore also turned them into marital issues.

Through therapy, Ron came to realize he was responsible for his neurotic need for peace. He learned it was his responsibility to understand why he had certain feelings and to see his psychological goal was illogical. While in therapy, Susan also came to realize the same was happening with her personal expectations and needs. Prior to these realizations, they both had the tendency to believe something was wrong with their marriage. In order to avoid putting all problems into the marital bucket, it is mandatory that each partner, as with Ron and Susan, examine his or her own individual lifestyle first before presuming it is the fault of the marriage.

Be Aware of Changing Scripts

As we've observed before, most couples entering therapy in an attempt to resolve specific issues are unaware that the marital problems they are having are a direct result of the lifestyle partnerships they formed at the beginning of their relationships. Remember, no couple can possibly form a union that is totally healthy. Therefore, the initial goal of marital therapy is to get each person to take responsibility for both his or her healthy and unhealthy approaches to life. The next step is to take responsibility for the healthy and unhealthy reasons the person married his or her partner and connected with specific lifestyle patterns. Once this is accomplished, the person can begin to see his or her present marital problems from an entirely different perspective. Most marital issues are lifestyle issues and each partner must learn to be responsible for his or her own personal approach to life. Specifically, this means owning both healthy and unhealthy response systems.

This awareness by both partners is especially necessary when one or both spouses go through changes within the marriage. No one stays the same through an entire marriage. Depending on numerous variables, each partner grows and develops into a creative person or becomes further entrenched in his or her neurotic solution where there is little chance for growth. These changes, viewed in terms of becoming healthy or unhealthy, can be referred to as the changing of the script.

Think of a marriage as a play, where each partner is an actor playing a specific role. There are marriages where both partners remain in their roles throughout the marriage. They never challenge themselves to grow and develop further. They repeat their roles over and over. Even though this is not considered healthy, these couples do not have to be concerned with the changing of scripts.

All come into the marriage with specific emotional needs. Therefore we choose partners who will allow us to continue with our planned routes. As a result of this selection process, both partners become part of a personal and unique play called marriage.

Each person marries for concrete psychological reasons and chooses a partner who has certain characteristics, ways of behaving and a specific role to play. Often, one or both partners become stuck in their roles trying to fulfill their neurotic needs. They play out their parts day after day, reinforced by their own intrinsic needs and by the demands and needs of their partners.

The dynamics and the interactions involved in a marital play are never a guarantee to remain the same throughout the entire marriage. When there is a role change by either partner, it can be a positive change where one partner becomes healthier or a negative change where one partner falls deeper into the neurotic track. When it is a positive change, it is because one partner has become tired and frustrated with the ill effects of the negative lifestyle and desires to grow and become healthier. When it is for negative reasons, the partner increases the intensity of his or her unhealthy solution hoping it will fulfill his or her personal psychological needs with more success.

These role changes often create problems. Regarding the change for the positive in one partner, it is good for a person to grow and develop. Yet it can still create a crisis in the marriage. Imagine that for years both partners play their particular roles in a marriage, perhaps part healthy and part unhealthy. Each partner becomes accustomed to the other's particular role and acclimates to whatever the role is. Now, after years of performing in one type of "play", one of the partners changes his or her role and therefore changes the script of the marriage. If the other partner is not adaptable to this change, it easily becomes a marital crisis.

The changing of scripts can provoke major problems in a marital relationship. A lack of understanding and adjustment by the other partner becomes a disaster in role interaction. This lack of adjustment to the changing of the script by one partner becomes a serious reason for the lack of success of so many marriages, especially in long-term ones. In the next example we observe one partner who grew in the relationship and another partner who did not.

Patricia's Story

Patricia, in her forties, came to therapy with a few marital problems but mainly wanted to discuss some personal issues going on in her life. She explained she was having thoughts and feelings she never had before. Some of these feelings were causing her to be upset and even afraid.

Patricia revealed she was beginning to like herself as a person and wanted to be around people who liked and appreciated her as well. In the past, she explained, she considered herself as a nonentity and was prepared to settle for a mediocre life.

At an early age she married Sam, a Marine in a handsome uniform. He represented power and security to her. Seeing herself as fragile and without talent, she neurotically, at least in part, chose a person she thought could protect her from anything that might expose her vulnerability. She walked up the aisle as a little girl going to her protector.

Patricia, with a great deal of introspection, realized she never asked much from her husband. In the initial years of marriage, she presumed she did not deserve anything special and was content with being safe and free of worry. With her feelings of inferiority always in the forefront, she felt unqualified to seek a man with expansive qualities. In reflection, she realized this type of man scared and overwhelmed her. She simply looked for what seemed like strength and was attracted to that characteristic.

After several years of marriage, her life began to change. It was far from sudden and took years for the pieces to come together. Nonetheless, a process of growth began to take place. My fearful client went back to school. She found it so rewarding, she did not stop with college but continued on to get her master's degree. Then she began to teach at the college level and was constantly stimulated by the environment and the people she met. She enjoyed the various groups with which she was involved and the members in return encouraged her to continue to grow and make use of the talents she had. As time passed, she was no longer the fragile little girl who chose to marry the strong looking Marine.

The same growth did not take place with her husband, Sam. He was a nice person, but he never grew out of the small world he lived in as a teenager. Once out of the Marines, he took a mundane job that did not require a college education. He had very few interests. He never expanded his world nor did he challenge himself to go beyond this level.

Patricia, now a much different person, came home from a stimulating work atmosphere feeling fulfilled. It could involve an interesting day or lunch with a dynamic friend. On many occasions, upon entering her home, she found her husband sprawled on the couch watching television with a can of beer resting on his camel-like stomach. The changing of the script had left them worlds apart.

Patricia, through a number of conversations, clearly saw what happened to her marriage, even though it took years to materialize. As their twenty-eighth anniversary approached, she had not come to any conclusion as to what to do and felt she needed time to make a very difficult decision.

In part 2, we have focused on formulating a definitive list of the primary reasons why many marriages fail and why many couples lead lives filled with tension and conflict even after years of marriage. The issues discussed entail the differences between having a good and healthy match versus a poor and unhealthy one. We discussed the importance of knowing what attracts us to specific partners. Most especially, it emphasizes the fact that it always involves both the healthy and unhealthy solutions. It warns of the dangers of putting too much in the marital bucket and the importance of facing life's problems for what they actually are, meaning not automatically a relationship problem. Finally, it reminds us that marriages are never stagnant. Over years of being together, both partners have the potential for changing for the better or for the worse. Even when these changes are for the better, it is the responsibility of each partner to adapt to the changes in order to keep the partnership one of cooperation and love.

We now understand the reality that no one partner uses the healthy solution all the time. Therefore, it logically follows that we spend time on our neurotic tracks in order to be free of anxiety or fear. Given this notion of our human imperfections, it also follows that any decision we make is never made for perfectly healthy reasons. It is reasonable for all of us to hope that the underlying reasons for any of our decisions comes primarily from our healthy tracks, but we still have to admit that some of the rationale for a decision comes from unhealthy reasoning, namely the desire to avoid feeling inferior or vulnerable.

Part Three

Making the Divorce Decision

As witnessed in unions of twenty-five years or more, marriages can endure for years with conflict and discord. However, as many eventually discover after years of dissatisfaction, hurt and sorrow, the time spent without a healthy resolution has led to a sham of two lives.

Those who stay in unhappy and destructive marital relationships for years give numerous reasons. Perhaps it is the desire to protect the children or it is due to finances and the need to evade further debt. Maybe there are religious reasons or the wish to avoid the stigma of being divorced. Whatever the reasons are on the surface, as true as some of them may be, there is a more accurate explanation that is rarely considered.

Many people are terrified to come to terms with who they truly are. They bypass the challenge of looking deeply into their lives in fear of facing the possible reality that their lives lack meaning and purpose. Too many marital relationships seem void of introspection. By ignoring certain realities about themselves, these spouses live in the hope that their marriages will stay intact. Analogously, we know we are going to die someday, but most avoid all discussions of the topic as if avoidance will delay its occurrence. Similarly, many know they are terribly unhappy in their relationships with their spouses, but they fear the consequences of facing the truth. They know that love is no longer part of the equation. Distance has replaced intimacy. They know this while riding in their cars alone, sitting in their homes and listening to love songs or observing what they are missing when watching romantic movies. Or more terrifyingly true, they know the reality of their feelings while lying in bed next to their spouses. The panic involved in change silences their realizations.

Most people, especially without a commitment to reflection and study, never reach an understanding about why their relationships with their spouses are not working. In conversations with friends, passing comments are often voiced, such as:

- "I can never please her. Complaining is in her blood."
- "He never communicates. He just doesn't get it."
- "Spend, spend, spend. I'm trying to keep her happy."
- "We have nothing in common. He goes his way; I go mine."
- "I would never marry the same person again."

Some comments are stated lightly, as if commenting on the weather. Others speak of multiple hurts and still others are said with underlying harshness, filled with anger and frustration. There's a pause, perhaps a nod of agreement from the listener and the subject is changed. It is the rare person who looks deeper at him or herself and the state of his or her marriage. Even with the slightest hint of awareness, the fear of recognition and absorbing the certainty of these kinds of remarks are all too overwhelming to face. Even after a divorce, the real reasons for the breakdown of relationships remain a mystery. As with the thoughts of death we spoke of earlier, there is the fear of the unknown.

For those married twenty to thirty years or more, crossing over to a new horizon, a new way of life, seems improbable and risky. For years these spouses do not view divorce as a solution to their isolation and loneliness. If the thought of splitting up with their spouses does cross their minds or even if it is said out loud, the fear of change erases it as an option. Many opt for the status quo, choosing to spend years in draining and destructive relationships. They ignore the fact, the real possibility, that the relationship could end with the next explosive incident. Some of the fears are valid, but most are exaggerated. The real fear lies in personal change. It is empowered by not knowing there is another way to love and be loved.

Change, in any situation, is difficult. However, it is equally difficult, actually more so, to live with unhealthy solutions that are powerfully addictive and destructive. In the majority of marriages, there are two people who continually and obsessively make attempts to conquer individual feelings of inferiority and vulnerability. This obsessive attention to self takes priority over any care or concern for another. Selfishness overrides love. They do not realize what their illogical striving to avoid realization of their personal vulnerabilities is doing to them and the marriage.

Over the years their personal unhealthy solutions to life grow in intensity and slowly become the major part of the marital relationship. In the stories of the troubled relationships we've looked at earlier, we've seen when one or both spouses are driven to the achievement of specific psychological and emotional goals, the relationship they have with their spouses becomes a primary factor in the accomplishment of these goals. The self-centered and neurotic demands of one partner are expected to be met by all, most especially and most consistently by their spouses. Self-centered needs overtake genuine interest in the other, slowly but inevitably making the relationship into a one-sided event.

Jeremy's Story

Jeremy is an illustration of the sort of person who was addicted to achieving one primary psychological goal in everything he did. He first came to therapy for the reason many individuals do: the achieving of his goal was derailed by recent events in his life. During his first few sessions he cried heavily, filled with sadness and a deep depression. He also explained, "I have had a few panic attacks during the past week where I could hardly breathe."

Jeremy was forty-three years old, married fourteen years and had three children. After a few sessions, Jeremy presented six early recollections and a recurring dream. The early recollections revealed a deep fear of being put in an embarrassing position, a fear of new experiences and a number of events where he lost control and fell. His recurring dream involved lying on the beach when, without warning, a huge wave washed over him.

Jeremy progressed through his childhood developing a number of fears and anxieties. In response to an overwhelming sense of vulnerability, he formulated a psychological goal to always be strong, ignore all emotional or physical pain and refuse to admit to any fears or vulnerabilities. Jeremy had developed a method for going through life making every effort to adhere to his psychological goals. I explained Jeremy's lifestyle to him using the analogy of a Central Park horse:

> Jeremy, you are like a horse in Central Park. You lower your head, blinders on both sides of your eyes, and you trudge forward with the hope of not seeing or hearing anything that might frighten you. You seek to just blend in and incessantly work your way through life with a single-minded goal. As you block out the terror of pain and suffering, you also block out any experience of joy or personal satisfaction. This addictive psychological goal would still be working if it were not for the event you recently experienced.

Even though Jeremy's goal was unreasonable and unhealthy, he was able to somehow function within his psychological solution for many years until he personally experienced the air strikes of September 11, 2001. As occurred for many people there that day or watching the events on television, the witnessing of such an event left Jeremy terrorized and numb. His emotional blinders were torn away. Since his psychological goal was unattainable in witnessing this event, he emotionally fell apart. His marriage and his relationship with his children were feeling the effects of his breakdown. For many months, Jeremy had a hard time dealing with any type of pain or suffering, whether it was something very small or something significant. Because he spent years addicted to his psychological goals, he had never developed the ability to deal with certain realities of life.

The goal of achieving a pure feeling about oneself while denying any knowledge of inferiority can be addictive. What is mistakenly at stake is the entire self-worth of the individual, the striving to overcome inferior feelings in exchange for only positive feelings. Karen Horney expands on this point when she explains how the addiction "promises not only a riddance from his painful and unbearable feelings (feeling lost, anxious, inferior and divided), but in addition an ultimately mysterious fulfillment of himself and his life."[1] It is the error and critical misjudgment in thinking, promised by the attainment of idealized goals, that the majority of spouses spend years acting out in their relationships.

When death comes to a person in the early years of life, it is more shocking than in the later years. We expect death to happen to older people or to people in the midst of experiencing a long-term illness. It is somewhat the opposite expectation when it comes to divorce. Divorce in the early years of marriage seems more socially expected. In some cases, we are aware of problems before a marriage and therefore are not surprised when it ends after a few years. On the other hand, we presume that once a marriage gets through its problematic and critical first years, it might very well last forever.

We have witnessed during the past few years a number of public figures who have surprised us with the announcement they were divorcing. Perhaps the biggest surprise was the news that Al and Tipper Gore were separating. Given their public image both as individuals and as a couple, the presumption was they were happily married and working enthusiastically together on many projects. There were no previous indications for anyone to conclude otherwise. Yet, just shortly after celebrating their fortieth wedding anniversary, they mutually announced to the world their decision to end their marriage.

Unlike the Gores, the marriage of John and Elizabeth Edwards was a public tragedy put on display for all to see. The shocking political scandal occurred while Edwards was running for president. An illicit affair, a baby born out of wedlock, periods of denial and lying all took place while Elizabeth was dying of cancer.

The surprise ending of long-term marriages is certainly not limited to those in the limelight or to celebrities. There are many marriages that present a public face that is far different from what is taking place in the privacy of the couples' homes. Many couples are aware that their relationships are on fragile ground but choose to ignore this fact. Perhaps it is easier to initially close one's eyes to marital problems rather than find the courage to dig deeper and work at making the changes necessary to improve the marriage.

The Gores chose to keep their reasons private while the Edwardses were forced to respond to a media circus, similar to the one Tiger Woods faced when his marriage ended. In each circumstance, even with the exposure of affairs, the facts underlying the real reasons the marriages didn't work will probably never be known. Perhaps it was the striving for power and the distractions that come from fame. Or, like many couples, perhaps it was the hours spent working and separately focusing on individual projects. In doing so, little time is left for the nourishment of the relationship.

When a divorce occurs after years of marriage, like that of former vice president Al Gore and his wife, the typical reaction is one of confusion and dismay. Often this is followed by a long list of guesses as to why the divorce is happening. Debates are initiated and comments are made about the well-being of each partner. No matter the worth or validity of such conversations, the majority of people are still left with one question: What happened?

In this book I want to take the mystery out of why some long-term marriages succeed and others end up in divorce court. The foundation for this reasoning lies in how each human being handles his or her personal vulnerabilities and inferiorities and the solutions he or she creates in response to these feelings. Therefore, marital problems are individual problems first that eventually turn into relationship problems.

Death and divorce have something in common. Psychiatrist Elizabeth Kubler-Ross explains, in a five-step model, the experiences and responses people have when facing death. The stages include denial, anger, bargaining, depression and finally, acceptance.[2] They are not necessarily experienced in this order nor are all experienced by everyone in the same manner. The likelihood, however, is that the majority of people will experience each of these stages for at least a brief period of time.

The stages people go through facing death can also be applied to other experiences in life, such as major sickness or injury, burdens created by financial bankruptcy or involvement in a major catastrophe. Marriages also experience a number of crises throughout the relationship and some are destined to go through the crisis of divorce. Therefore, these specific stages, as set forth by Kubler-Ross, can also be applied not only to the challenges one goes through during a marriage, but also to the turmoil and uncertainty experienced by couples facing divorce.

M. Scott Peck reaches the same conclusion when he explains:

> Initially, as differences between partners emerge, our first tendency is to try to deny these differences and to deny that we have fallen out of love. When we can no longer deny that, we get angry at our spouse for being different from us. When that doesn't get us anywhere and our spouse doesn't change, we try to bargain in some manner or another. When that doesn't work, we become depressed and the marriage looks very doubtful.[3]

The longer in years that a deficient and defective marriage goes on, the longer and more painful time spent in each of these stages. Likewise, the longer it takes for one or both partners to come to terms with the reality of divorce, the more one is likely to struggle and become stuck in one of these stages for extended periods of time.

When these stages occur within a marriage, it is mandatory that the stage of acceptance be reached in order for the marriage to return to a healthy relationship and remain there. Acceptance requires that each spouse recognize and accept his or her addiction to an unhealthy solution and then choose not to live within it.

The same goal of acceptance needs to be reached by those experiencing a separation that is leading to a divorce. As these partners experience each of these stages, the final stage needs to be reached for them to proceed with their individual lives in a healthier manner. Adler explains, "For the neurotic, coming to understand his own picture of the world— a picture which he built up early in childhood and which has served his 'private map', so to speak, for making his way through life—is an essential part of the cure."[4] As seen in previous case histories, there are many divorce situations where one or both partners get stuck in certain stages (often anger or depression) and never reach the stage of acceptance.

Denial

No one gets married thinking about divorce. Sometimes there is little thought of divorce during the first years of marriage when children are born, homes are bought and careers are being developed. However, this phase of marriage comes and goes quickly and the routine of marriage sets in. During the next phase of the marriage, if it has not already happened, problems and challenges in the relationship begin to surface. Having problems and challenges in the relationship does not mean there is something wrong with the marriage, but they do require responses that are healthy and creative.

The challenges a husband and wife experience will affect each of them differently. At the same time, they will not have the same approach or solution in responding to the challenge, be it healthy or unhealthy. When problems do arise, the primary consideration for both partners is to realize and admit that it is always a possibility for them to use their unhealthy solutions as responses. Denying this possibility is the first step toward making the relationship unhealthy. Unhealthy solutions are dictated by one's selfish need to avoid all forms of vulnerability. They have nothing to do with responding to the challenge logically and certainly have nothing to do with mutual cooperation.

Therefore, it is a mistake not to think about how any relationship can become increasingly unhealthy. Denying the thought of a relationship becoming unhealthy or even ending in divorce also leaves the outcome up to whim and circumstance. It takes courage to face this possibility in marriage, but in not doing so we are left in a state of ignorance. Keeping a relationship simple and not seeing it for its possible complications is risky at best. The lack of thinking in depth eventually leads to more trouble not only for the one partner in denial, but also for the relationship itself. Whether it is because of laziness, fear or personal pride, by not taking the time to examine our own biases in response to challenges, we lose the opportunity to see if a relationship is becoming unhealthy and the ways we can make it better.

The statistics in marriage are not very promising. There are not many things we would venture into if there was only a 50 percent chance for the possibility of success. As if in denial of these statistics, too many individuals in relationships are never willing to see the possibility of divorce happening to them. Denial is one definitive reason for the percentages of divorce remaining so high.

Alex and Bridget's Story

Alex was aware that his relationship with Bridget was in a tumultuous state. Desiring to keep the family together at all costs, he fell into the habit of using quick fixes for problems as they occurred. He knew Bridget had a damaged ego that revealed its fragility on a regular basis. She was always in the shadow of her older brother and experienced embarrassment and humiliation at the hands of her mother. As a result of childhood experiences, Bridget entered her adult life severely lacking in self-worth. As the years of marriage went on, it increasingly became Alex's job to act as a buffer to all outside events and people who might arouse Bridget's extremely low self-esteem. He took on the responsibility as her partner for inflating her ego wherever and whenever it was possible. Knowing he was simply surviving the relationship rather than living in it, he pretended that the end goal justified the means and tactics he was using for the purpose of keeping the family together.

In addition to protecting Bridget from outside forces that might tap her sensitivities, Alex also had to deal with the lifestyle solution Bridget had developed as a defense system for herself. There were times when Bridget revealed herself as a master in achieving her emotional goals. Over time, she had developed characteristics and traits that were often used to perfection in striving to reach the ideal picture she wanted to achieve and have others see. Bridget's actions can be understood through Horney's explanation of this type of person: "He is often charming indeed, particularly when new people come into the orbit. Regardless of their factual importance for him, he *must* impress them. He gives the impression to himself and others that he 'loves' people."[5] Alex was fully aware that to outsiders Bridget was viewed as loving and giving. He was actually content, neurotic as it may seem, with this picture people had of her, for it took some of the burden off him in supplying her addictive needs.

Even with Bridget's talents for fulfilling her emotional needs with outsiders, keeping her sense of self-importance at a high level became an increasingly difficult task. By the time his marriage reached its twenty-fifth year, Alex had become extremely frustrated and eventually depressed over the situation in his marriage. He fully realized the immense task presented to him on a daily basis. Keeping Bridget fulfilled and happy became more and more difficult. Behind closed doors, Bridget's complaining about her so-called unfulfilled life grew in intensity. Alex was the target of her anger and wrath for not supporting her emotional demands. Wherever they lived or wherever they went, Alex was castigated and rebuked for Bridget's sense of unhappiness.

As Alex's two children grew older, they became aware of their mother's demanding needs. In increased fashion, one or the other often asked their father, "Is there anything that makes Mom happy?" Alex denied the implications of the question and told them they had to respect their mother. In steady acts of denial, he fooled himself and tried to fool his children into thinking things would improve. When Bridget's explosions became more frequent, Alex was faced with other comments from his children, who were also dragged into playing the same role as their father. Frustrated by their own failures to please their mother, they asked their father, "How do you put up with this?" Remaining committed to his unhealthy emotional goals, Alex again denied what he knew to be true and returned to the task of trying to keep Bridget fulfilled.

This act of denial also allowed outsiders to be fooled into judging Alex and Bridget as a "happy and loving couple." After years of outsiders experiencing what they thought was a true picture of Alex and Bridget's marriage, no one had the slightest clue of what was taking place when Alex and Bridget were alone. In these times, rarely was there a moment of peace. Every car ride, every walk on the beach and every weekend were filled with complaints and criticism. As Bridget's anger increased, Alex's depression deepened. Alex's periods of denial swept away the hidden realities of their marriage.

As the marriage approached its twentieth year, Alex was the target of Bridget's ongoing disapproval and badgering. Almost every time they were alone together, more and more complaints and criticism surfaced. Alex kept these ongoing attacks to himself, hoping to shield his two children from the state of the marriage. The final crisis arose when the children became targets for similar aggression and hostility. Alex's years of denial were falling apart as his family became more and more divided. No one wanted to come home, including Alex. Both he and his children nervously entered the front door never knowing Bridget's mood of the day. There might be days when Bridget was on a high because of some outside event. These were called "good" days by Alex and his children, respites from doom and gloom and occasions for him to pretend all was well. Alex's ongoing denial continued for just so long, though. He soon became another divorce statistic.

In individual and marital therapy, I explain to clients the psychological fact that what people try to avoid they end up creating. By way of example, I discuss Jim, the student whom we spoke of earlier, who mistakenly saw himself as being unable to meet the academic demands of school. As a result of this conviction, he did little in terms of homework or preparing for tests. He avoided these tasks so as not to expose his perceived notion that he was stupid, thereby hoping to avoid even further humiliation. Over the years of schooling, the consequences of his behavior reached a conclusion. As he was doing everything possible not to expose his supposed ignorance, he actually became ignorant through his lack of effort. He created what he was trying to avoid.

The psychologically intelligent and healthy individual recognizes she has strengths and weaknesses, talents and limitations. She has enough common sense to know she is not perfect, nor can she solve every challenge with excellence. With this knowledge and attitude, this individual has the courage to reexamine perceptions developed in childhood and to judge whether they are actually true or are basic misconceptions that require major revisions. Jim, the young student, never gave himself this opportunity. By not accepting the reality that all people are imperfect, he denied himself the opportunity to discover whether his supposed ignorance was true or might be an error in judgment. In denial and focusing on what he perceived as a major limitation, he wasted numerous years in safeguarding the experience of this inferiority.

Of the five stages Kubler-Ross presents, denial is perhaps the one both partners spend the most time experiencing as they face the daily challenges of their marriage. The extended length of time is especially true in marriages of twenty or more years. The longer one is married, the longer time for the possibility of denial.

In my experience as a therapist, I have found that no one who initiates marital therapy discusses his or her present situation for very long. As soon as I ask spouses when they think their marital problems began, they always go back to the very beginning of the marriage. A particular event might have caused the couple to come to therapy, but it is as if the partners know the real underlying problems were always present and operating for a long time. The acts of denial kept them from coming for help.

Couples also come to therapy after years of living with the consequences of an unhealthy psychological approach to life. By denying core feelings about themselves and their relationships with their spouses, partners are actually making matters worse than they need to be. As with individual behavior, couples fall into the same trap. What couples try to avoid, they create. The act of denial leads to further problems, creates unhealthier people and eventually leads to unhealthier marriages. Now let's look more deeply at how partners can be in denial for much of their marriage, with one partner remaining stuck in denial even during the divorce.

Cynthia and Stan's Story

Cynthia and Stan were married for twenty years when they first went for marriage counseling. Cynthia felt the marriage was over but for her own private intentions decided to give marriage counseling a try. She chose the therapist and made the first appointment with me.

Cynthia took over the first session by explaining Stan's long list of problems. Stan remained quiet and was not surprised at the list. He had heard the accusations for years. He was aware of the direction the marriage had taken and that the relationship between the two of them was deteriorating at an overwhelming speed. However, he had no idea how to stop the downfall. Therefore, at the initial marriage counseling session, he knew he had to admit to all the faults listed by Cynthia, real or not, for the marriage counseling to continue.

I often tell clients that no one leaves his or her lifestyle—his or her approach to life's challenges—in the waiting room. Clients bring, for the most part unaware, their basic methods of operation right into the sessions. Cynthia was in denial of her role in the condition of the marriage and its being unhealthy. She never considered that her approach to the relationship with Stan might be permeated by her need never to feel inferior or inadequate. Living in denial, she unwittingly brought her unhealthy solution to marriage counseling.

In the second session, Cynthia brought in index cards and explained to me, "I do not want to forget anything. Sometimes my memory is not that good." Not realizing her neurotic lifestyle pattern, she came prepared with another arsenal of demeaning statements about her husband. She read her list of Stan's faults and described situations in the recent past to confirm her perspective. She emphasized each point, "He's a control freak. He always thinks he is right. He is emotionally abusive. I think he has a chemical imbalance. He's an alcoholic." As the list became lengthier, I interrupted and asked Stan if he had a drinking problem. It was time for Stan to confess his sins. He responded, "There are times I overdrink. Most of the time, however, I think I can control it. I probably do have the alcoholic gene." I asked him if he thought he could stop and Stan said he would, especially if it helped the marriage.

As Cynthia continued with her list, Stan tried to interject by asking, "Do *you* have any faults or is this all about me?" He knew full well, without need for an answer, that each marriage counseling session would be all about him. This was the course his marriage had increasingly taken over the last twenty years. Especially during the past five years, as the marital problems intensified, Stan tried his best to ignore the harsh realities of his marriage. His solution became routine: just admit to being wrong so as to stop the fighting. He was choosing to reach some sort of peace, knowing the love between him and Cynthia would never return. Once again, without consciously being aware of his actions, Stan was a partner in creating what he desperately was trying to avoid.

During the third session, I asked Cynthia if there was anything she liked about Stan. I went on, "Do you want marriage counseling? Do you love this person? Is there anything you like about him?" Cynthia, unaware as to why I asked these questions, responded without hesitation, "I think I still love him. But he has to change. He has so much to change." Stan was mystified about what to say.

Toward the end of the session, Stan informed me that Cynthia had filed for divorce. Surprised, I turned to Cynthia and asked, "How can you be getting marriage counseling and divorcing Stan at the same time? You have to decide what you want. You can't be trying to resolve marital issues and filing for divorce at the same time." I saw these two behaviors as contradictions. I did not realize that in one way they were not. Cynthia's long list of berating remarks written on index cards served the purpose of getting Stan to shape up. Cynthia probably was thinking, *It worked for years. Why not now?* Serving the divorce papers served the same purpose. *Knock him down and get him to crawl back.*

Stan knew this feedback from me to his wife would be a problem. Actually, he knew it would be a disaster. Over the years he saw how Cynthia responded to someone who confronted her or disagreed with her. When he returned for the fourth counseling session, Cynthia was not there. I informed him that Cynthia had telephoned me right after the previous session and left an angry message. Cynthia had said in the message, "You don't get it. You don't understand me. I am angry that you have not listened to me at all."

I explained to Stan that I had called Cynthia several times, but she never returned my calls. I was genuinely confused and did not immediately realize the reasons underlying Cynthia's bizarre behavior until later. Cynthia was incapable of having honest communication. Without such honesty, the chances for therapy diminished as well. As Karen Horney explains, "The most relevant question in this regard is: how deeply entrenched are the trends, and how great is the incentive or potential incentive to outgrow them?"[6] From Cynthia's perspective, she was sure she had nothing to outgrow. It was Stan who needed to change.

Stan explained to me that what I had experienced with Cynthia was a small example of what he had experienced over the last twenty years. Stan told me he was embarrassed by the exposure of his sheepish behavior during the entire marriage. He realized, finally, that his twenty years of denial had to stop. Silently, though, he wondered if Cynthia had not filed for divorce, would he have had the courage to stop the emotionally destructive behavior himself? He was forced to be honest with his own thoughts. He knew, as horrible as it was to admit, he would have continued with his lifestyle of denial. Ironically, therefore, Cynthia's filing for divorce became a gift of freedom for Stan to get on a healthy track. His decades of a self-imposed prison sentence were over. Now he had to learn the art of being healthy.

Stan's years of denial are far from unusual. Unhealthy marriages last for years due to at least one partner being stuck in denial. There are times when a partner like Stan experiences the angry stage, but it is short-lived. A person with Stan's lifestyle cannot afford to stay in the angry stage for long, for it goes against his emotional need to stay connected to his or her spouse and keep the marriage going. Stan fell deeper into his unhealthy track in order to appease the neurotic demands of his wife. He was losing his identity and could not afford to be himself. To keep the marriage going, he had to be what Cynthia wanted for herself.

As a result, depression is more likely the stage in which a partner with Stan's lifestyle might spend a great deal of time wallowing. There will be times of bargaining (promising to be better), only to be followed by a return to the platform of denial and depression.

The only true solution for all unhealthy marriages is to reach the final stage of acceptance. To stop the denying and to get relief from the depression, the realities of the individual lifestyle patterns and of the marriage need to be addressed. In Stan's marriage, he was pushed into this final stage. If it were not for Cynthia filing for divorce and refusing marriage counseling, Stan still might be stuck in the stages of denial or depression.

Cynthia and Stan were copartners in denial. As Stan ignored the realities of their destructive relationship, Cynthia fed on it. She consistently used intimidation with Stan as a means for avoiding anything that might crush her pride. Karen Horney succinctly describes the goals of this type of lifestyle by explaining, "They try to achieve such mastery in different ways: by self-admiration and the exercise of charm; by compelling fate through the height of their standards; by being invincible and conquering life in the spirit of a vindictive triumph."[7]

Cynthia's vindictiveness became the main force in her marriage. Stan was demeaned for his so-called failures on a regular basis, not only as a husband but as a father as well. Even if the failures were true and Stan admitted to mistakes, Cynthia reveled in reminding him of his faults and inadequacies. Cynthia did not see her behavior as being vindictive. Without any awareness, Cynthia ultimately created, over a period of twenty years of marriage, what she was trying desperately to avoid. As a wife and mother, she would now experience the pains of no longer being admired or loved.

Anger and Depression

Anger is more likely to take place in the partner who is using the expansive or narcissistic solution. Depression is more likely to be accompanied by the use of the self-effacing solution. The narcissists are more active in their demands, while self-effacing types tend to be passive. As we saw in the marriage of Cynthia and Stan, Cynthia spent the three sessions of marital counseling spewing her anger at her husband. There was no introspection on her part. She said she loved Stan, but he had many changes to make. Karen Horney, in discussing the narcissistic solution, states that this type can easily become vindictive: "He feels rather that his needs or his tasks are so important that they entitle him to every privilege. He does not question his rights and expects others to love him unconditionally, no matter how much he actually trespasses on their rights."[8] Cynthia spent three sessions pontificating on how her demands were not met. Stan only experienced her love if he followed her demands and expectations without any hesitation.

Cynthia's anger turned into a vindictive mind-set. Throughout the marriage, Stan experienced her outbursts and fits of anger when she did not get what she wanted. M. Scott Peck explains this type of rage: "The anger center in humans works in exactly the same way as it does in other creatures. It is basically a territorial mechanism, firing off when any other creature impinges on our territory."[9] In this situation, the territory was Cynthia's life track that was not to be interfered with, certainly not without expecting a strong reaction. Her anger level intensified and came at a greater pace as their marriage entered its twentieth year. His response, self-effacing as he was, was filled with promises to meet her needs the next time. The marriage reached a point where Cynthia's anger, more often than not, succeeded in making Stan's responses ones of subdued appeasement.

The demands became more outlandish and unpredictable. It became impossible for Stan to succeed in pleasing her at every turn. Cynthia continued to refuse any level of introspection. Not aware of the extent of her own neurotic needs and demands, there were moments when she raised her anger to another level. Horney explains these increased stages of anger: "When they are not fulfilled there ensues a punitive vindictiveness which may run the whole gamut."[10] Stan's final punishment was the divorce papers.

The anger stage Kubler-Ross defines is certainly evident in many marriages. Without any attempt to change, this anger is often intensified during the divorce proceedings. While bringing anger to the divorce proceedings, the partner who remains seething in anger will often seek affirmation for his or her feelings of irritation and rage. As partners remain in this stage for an extended period of time, they typically begin to share their anger toward their spouses with others. As a result, they will often attract and be supported by those stuck in the anger stage themselves. Not only is this true of the friends with whom they choose to associate during this stage, but it also actually influences the type of lawyers they will retain for the divorce.

Surrounding yourself with people who agree with you is certainly not unusual, especially for those using their unhealthy solutions in response to life's problems. Neurotics continually look to have their illogical reasoning affirmed and seek to have their anger justified. In many cases, one or both partners get divorced using the same solutions they employed within the marriage. The narcissist or expansive type has the tendency to be filled with anger and is often on the attack. The self-effacing type is more likely to be depressed and more passive during the divorce process.

I often explain to clients who are being inundated with angry accusations they must make an attempt to see the big picture. I remind them that the rage that is being directed toward them is nothing new, for they experienced the same behavior in marriage. I have to remind them that the abuse they have become the targets of now that divorce is taking place is one of the main reasons they are ending the relationships in the first place.

The narcissistic partners, especially the ones still stuck in the angry and vindictive stage, seek lawyers who are also angry. A good number of them tend to be narcissistic and furious people themselves and use the divorce process as a platform for their ingrained anger. Narcissistic lawyers love power and, like abusive marriage partners, are ready to use it. One can only imagine what these lawyers' marriages are like.

There is a much more civil approach to getting a divorce. It is referred to in the legal profession as Collaborative Law. This approach takes into consideration the fact that both partners are entering the divorce process with a vast array of emotions, including anger and depression. With the agreement of both partners, lawyers using the collaborative method approach the divorce with mutual respect for both partners. They deal primarily with the facts and realities of the situation and leave much of the destructive emotions out of the discussion. After a fair negotiation, the results are mutually accepted by both partners and the final stage of divorce (acceptance) is reached in less time, is far less expensive and certainly ends more peacefully.

The Collaborative Law approach has no benefit for the partner or lawyer stuck in the angry stage. Nor does it fit the needs of either of them when they are still using the expansive solution (control and domination) to meet their narcissistic needs. Such a partner feels strongly that someone must be at fault for the relationship ending and uses the divorce process and the appropriate lawyer to satisfy his or her inferior needs and accomplish his or her neurotic goals. As tragic as some divorces are, they become more so with the actions of such partners and lawyers who need to have a battle to express their power, regain control and win the contest. A partner gives many bullets to the lawyer, whether they are exaggerated or false, and the lawyer fires away. The lawyer, in fact, might very well add a few bullets to keep the battle going. In the end, there are no winners, except the lawyer who walks away with a nice paycheck. One can believe the lawyer deposits the check conscience-free for, as with the partner he or she served, there is little in terms of conscience.

Some people mistakenly presume that the unhealthy behavior will cease once the divorce papers are served. Unless there is a strong effort by either partner to change the lifestyle solutions that led to the failure of the marriage, the partners are more than likely to bring these same solutions to the divorce proceedings. Marital problems are always individual problems first and while married, many partners refuse to evaluate the ways their approaches to life are unhealthy, thereby repeating those mistakes during the divorce.

Deirdre and Dominic's Story

Deirdre, in her late forties, initiated therapy with a great deal of stress, hopelessness and fear. She explained she was married for almost thirty years to an older man. Her husband, Dominic, now eighty, brought Deirdre from Europe to America when she was eighteen and hired her as a nanny for his three children. Although Dominic was married at the time, they began to have a relationship during the first year. Dominic then divorced his wife and married Deirdre.

The marriage was physically and emotionally abusive from the beginning. Dominic was a multi-millionaire who obtained his wealth both legally and illegally. In therapy, Deirdre did not need to be told that she had made a terrible mistake in marrying Dominic. She described herself as being a fragile and frightened young woman. Lost and confused and in search of a secure situation, she put all her trust in what she thought was a fatherly figure. Deirdre was still lost and confused, but she knew she had to get out of this terrifying situation.

Deirdre found a lawyer she felt she could trust and began the divorce process. As expected, her husband exploded when he received the legal papers. Up to this point in the twenty-eight-year marriage, he ran the household, especially his wife, with an iron and bullying fist. It was one of the first times someone confronted him and he immediately started on the attack with threats and intimidation. The so-called bullets he and his lawyer used were filled with half-truths and in many cases blatant lies.

Dominic's lawyer saw from the beginning the amount of money involved in the divorce. Deirdre was asking for very little, primarily seeking peace and her freedom. Dominic, tortured by his loss of power, was willing to spend any amount in revenge. He sought to destroy Deirdre one way or another. His lawyer became a willing, narcissistic and angry co-conspirator. The lawyer had three million dollars of Dominic's money put in escrow, of which the lawyer alone had control. Revealing his pathology, Dominic's lawyer was overheard saying to Deirdre's lawyer, "I don't care about this creep. Let's keep this thing going so we can take him for all he's worth." Two angry and self-consumed narcissists were playing their power cards. Dominic, immersed in the foolishness of his lifestyle solution, unknowingly became the victim of his lawyer's greed.

Deirdre, noticeably self-effacing, was able to survive a tedious and long divorce. She, like other self-effacing personality types, did not see anger as her right. In the self-effacing drive to be loved, accepted and approved of, all the expansive characteristics are avoided. As Horney explains, "While curtailed in any pursuit on his own behalf, he is not only free to do things for others but, according to his inner dictates, should be the ultimate of helpfulness, generosity, considerateness, understanding, sympathy, love and sacrifice."[11] Due to this ingrained passivity, Deirdre was barely able to defend herself, even when being treated in an insulting way. Feeling inferior already, the attacks and accusations from others simply reinforced her original convictions about herself. The marriage ended after years of confrontation. Dominic and his lawyer, still filled with rage and vindictiveness, would be in search of another victim.

Bert and Diane's Story

Bert and Diane were married for thirty-five years when Diane followed through on years of threats and filed for divorce. Bert was well aware that his relationship with Diane had become filled with tension and long periods of silence. He felt guilty that he was most happy when he was away from her. If she went on a trip, he happily had a week without being demeaned or humiliated. Communication was never part of the relationship. The marriage was all about Diane, with hardly any space for Bert's concerns.

During the first six months of separation, Bert fell into a deep depression. The depression was a continuation of the previous two years of his marriage, but during this time his world became even darker. He was not crying over the end of the marriage, for that was more of a relief. The tears, at times coming with heavy sobbing, were over a sense of hopelessness and failure. Lacking the courage to leave, he had been trying to keep the marriage together for over twenty years. When his wife found out he was often in tears, she commented to one of her children, "Good! That means he still cares." Once again it was all about her, void of any feeling for a man she claimed to have loved.

Bert and Diane's financial situation had reached rock bottom. They were in massive debt and the house had to be sold. Another shattered dream, exploding in Bert's face, brought on a deeper depression. Bert had envisioned his home filled with grandchildren someday, truly a light at the end of a long and dark marital tunnel. Knowing he could not afford an expensive divorce, Bert sought a lawyer specializing in Collaborative Law. He wanted both of them to come away equally with something, as little as that might be.

In what was referred to as a four-way, Bert and Diane met with their lawyers. It was agreed that the divorce would proceed using the collaborative approach, thus avoiding the expense of an unnecessary trial. Diane was not happy with some of the decisions made in the first meeting and considered firing her lawyer. The expansiveness of her narcissistic nature had her convinced she would become wealthy without lifting a finger. Her lawyer went along with the collaborative procedure at first but knew full well she would have to appease Diane in the process.

Some divorce lawyers, like Diane's, have to give some reason, as false as it may be, to compensate for the money they intend to make. Due to both Diane's and her lawyer's neurotic needs, anger and fighting were all they knew.

During the first six months of separation, the bills and expenses were overwhelming. Diane was still not working and had no intention of doing so. Bert, still fighting depression, was given the unexpected news that he needed $25,000 worth of dental work done. Searching for some sort of reprieve from this additional financial crisis, he requested through his lawyer that Diane consider helping out with the expenses.

Bert was not surprised by Diane and her lawyer's response. For years he had witnessed friends who were forced to deal with lawyers who brought their pathological anger into their practices. They preyed on naïve clients who were also angry, making promises that had only one purpose: to keep the money flowing. Diane and her lawyer's reply to Bert's appeal hit an all-time low. In response to Bert's plea for help, they said, "Perhaps he can conserve costs by just having all his teeth pulled. That shouldn't cost much."

Once again, Bert was not surprised by their audacity and insolence. Their disrespect for the welfare of another exemplified their self-centered lifestyles. What did surprise him was that they were foolish enough to put it in writing. Neither of them cared about the dental situation Bert was forced to face. Once again, it was all about them. Dr. Peck notes with clarity the foundation for such behavior. He explains, "The tendency to avoid problems and the emotional suffering inherent in them is the primary basis of all psychological illnesses."[12] Diane and her lawyer, blinded by their narcissistic needs, presumed there were riches waiting for them at the end.

One good thing did come about as a result of Diane and her lawyer resorting to their vindictive rage and anger. It woke up the sleeping lion and Bert was able to move out of the depressive stage in which he was stuck. He moved to the final stage of acceptance with the full realization that his divorce was an opportunity for a return to the healthy path.

Bargaining

Bargaining is a stage to which many people turn when facing death once they have ceased denying the finality of their situations and their anger or depression has subsided. The bargaining stage is also not uncommon in many marital situations. In most instances, it is only one partner who enters this area of behavior, while the other remains stuck in another. Perhaps after years of denying the reality of the relationship and after years of fighting and depression, one partner turns to another method in one last attempt to save the marriage. This does not mean he or she will not return to previous stages, for the pressures inherent in bargaining often create more depression or anger. Nonetheless, there are many marriages of over twenty years where one partner comes in and out of this stage on a regular basis. It is an attempt by the partner to do everything he or she can to appease his or her spouse and avoid the foreseeable reality of divorce.

In some marriages, bargaining can begin in the early stages of marriage. However, this stage is more likely to reveal itself after years of marriage and after all other methods have failed. Some may have tried counseling but were unsuccessful. Without full admission of their unhealthy approaches to their relationships, such couples often leave counseling resigned to the fate of their marriages. It is something spouses do not talk about with each other, as if hoping some magic cure will come along to mediate their situation. With neither one opting for divorce, at least for the time being, they return to the stages with which they are most comfortable. It is here where one partner, perhaps terrified of a divorce and in fear of its consequences, begins to meet his or her partner's demands in every way possible. In doing so, he or she sets the stage in survival mode.

Karen and Mike's Story

Karen and Mike came for marriage counseling in the middle of their seventeenth year of marriage. After attending a few sessions together, they requested individual sessions for a period of time. Karen felt she did not have enough time to express herself when they came together, while Mike felt uneasy about revealing his real thoughts in front of his wife. As is true in many marriage counseling situations, both Mike and Karen waited for a crisis to occur before seeking help.

Karen was convinced her husband was having an affair. Not concerned for the consequences of doing so, she called Mike's two immediate bosses to report to them this affair going on in their company. In essence, she was trying to get Mike reprimanded for his behavior or, perhaps, to teach him a lesson and get him fired. Karen was not positive Mike was having an affair but presumed it was linked to the lack of attention she was getting from him. It never occurred to her that his lack of attention might be due to her behavior in the relationship.

Karen admitted to experiencing a childhood without love or affection. She felt her mother was overwhelmed and did not really want children. She was always afraid her father was going to leave. She faintly admitted to this being the reason she never felt connected to Mike, but Karen emphasized, "Mike always needs someone to take care of him. He is not a good business partner. I know I am aggressive, but if he did more maybe I would be less demanding." Not realizing her perspective on the marriage might be illogical, she further explained, "I need someone to put me in check. I need a man who stands up to me. Mike never does, so I end up the bad guy."

Mike left the home while in counseling but returned after a week. He felt guilty about leaving his two young children. Mike explained that he no longer felt he could live with his wife but hated the thought of divorce and how it might affect the children. He explained, "I know I have a lot of resentment after so many years of living with her. Karen is very competent, but a great deal of time she is an abusive ruler. We do not match. I have become a conflict avoider. I am so tired of her criticism."

During one session, Karen said she felt she knew who she was, but it was too painful to face. In the same session, she explained, "I put on a mask of being tough. But Mike is so soft and into spiritual stuff. I think the marriage is over, but I am in no rush." Karen remained angry about Mike having a possible affair. She felt she could not get the truth out of him but would one way or another. Toward the end of the session she admitted to being lonely and sad. She clarified, "I don't miss Mike. I miss the life we could have had. I was raised to be strong. I only stayed this long not wanting to give up what we have."

After eight individual sessions, Mike decided to stop therapy for a while. He explained that he was going to try to make the marriage work. Karen wanted to move to a bigger house, so he felt this would keep her busy for a while. He knew the house was more than he could afford but believed his leaving the kids would create more problems.

The same scenario repeated itself five years later when both Karen and Mike returned to counseling. Nothing in the relationship had changed. They had moved to the new home and put an addition on three years previously. An oversized pool was built in the backyard. The tension between the two of them had increased. Mike spent his free time writing spiritual novels, which gave him a feeling of accomplishment. During one counseling session, Mike admitted to feeling depressed. He explained, "During the past five years, I have given her everything she asked for. But this past Saturday was horrible. We had another fight over nonsense and later I did not know what to do with myself. No matter what I do, she gives me the feeling that I don't belong." Once again, Mike was considering leaving the marriage.

Mike had spent the last five years in and out of the bargaining stage. He was going along with everything Karen wanted and never felt part of the decision-making process. Seeing that his efforts were useless, he found himself in the stage of depression more and more often. Mike was considering giving it one more chance, but deep down he knew his attempts to please Karen would be short-lived. Karen, feeling more content with her position in life, admitted that she no longer cared if Mike left. In her last session, she expressed confidently, "I know I am a good woman and mother. I can take care of myself and always have. Let's see if Mike can do without me." The marriage kept together within the bargaining stage was about to end.

Acceptance

Acceptance is the final stage in the model established by Kubler-Ross. In speaking of the necessity for courage in facing one's death, she notes, "Acceptance should not be mistaken for a happy stage. It is almost void of feelings. It is as if the pain had gone, the struggle is over, and there comes a time for 'the final rest before the long journey.'"[13] In the demise of marriages, the stage of acceptance occurs during the separation period and continues through and after the divorce. Full acceptance is a stage few are able to reach. But for those who do, there is the opportunity to move toward a new horizon.

During the divorce process, there is always doubt. Should this really happen? Should I try again? Maybe things will be different if we both try harder. Both partners, if they are being honest, know they could have done more to make the marriage work. The partners in divorce may wonder, *Why did I deny for so long? I was so foolish to have wasted so many years.*

Acceptance cannot overshadow the memories of marriage, such as the day partners knew they fell in love. Falling in love created its own energy, fueling the heart as never before. It was a time of conviction. With a sense of surety, there was the belief that nothing could impede the strength of their bond. The wedding day may be recalled. The birth of each child completed their union of love. More than just sex, they participated in creation. And then the question is asked, "What happened to the joy when we walked down the aisle or when we brought our children home?" The memories may fade slowly, but they never go away.

For many of the years people are married, each partner wastes time by believing problems can be ignored and love need not be nourished. In both physical and marital death, the question becomes *Should I hang on or let go?* Then the time comes when the fight for existence reaches its last heartbeat. There is relief in the thought the battles are over and that only peace lies ahead. The moments facing death are filled with terror but overflowing with hope. The death of a marital relationship often fills one with remorse but releases the hopeful spirit of what the future might be.

The acceptance of a marriage's death is certainly monumental, but just as in physical death, one senses when it is time to go. The communication has ceased; the love has become nonexistent. Holding on lacks logic and only offers more pain. Acceptance becomes the rightful alternative. It is the choice that brings hope of a new life ahead.

Healing After Divorce

In my dormitory room when I was at college, a wooden plaque hung on the wall with a quote from an anonymous writer reading, "In order to reach new horizons, one must leave the shore." Many couples spend years in disastrous and destructive relationships, too fearful to face the thoughts of uncertainty. They move back and forth in Kubler-Ross's stages of facing death—denial, anger, depression, bargaining—avoiding the last stage of acceptance out of fear of the unknown. They might know acceptance is the only chance to stop the hypocrisy and to move on to a more meaningful life but feel the task is overwhelming. Perhaps after years of marriage, with courage and fortitude, many do decide to leave the empty shore and begin the journey toward a new horizon. By the time the divorce is finalized, one or both partners know the courage it took to leave that with which they were familiar and to which they were accustomed.

Both deciding to change the direction of a conflict-ridden marriage or taking all the steps toward divorce take courage. Each partner, once he or she is through the emotional turmoil that comes with getting a divorce, needs to be aware that another challenge awaits. Courage is once again needed as partners face numerous issues following the decision to divorce. No one reaches the new horizon immediately. The saying on my dormitory wall, as powerful as it is, omits the reality that once we do leave the shore, there will be a period of time when we will be floating in a void. It takes time and a great deal of thought to learn the art of being healthy and to create a new life for oneself. It also takes time to create a new environment. It involves many decisions and a lot of work to break the habits formed while using our neurotic solutions.

There is a time period, both terrifying and lonely, when we might doubt our decisions to leave a marriage. We have left the safety and protection of routine, only to find ourselves in the middle of nowhere. With no quick answers at the forefront, it can be frightening and confusing. It can be a time when disastrous decisions are made. Good judgment is mandatory. As frightening as this stage can be and as much as we want our lives to be better, we owe it to ourselves to take time for reflection.

The days and months approaching divorce are crucial. They are often filled with anxiety, frustration and periods of anger. In the final days approaching the end of the marriage, both partners are usually drained and exhausted. I always tell clients, as resigned as they may feel, the day before the judge will still arouse a range of mixed feelings, including perhaps a sense of sadness. Neither partner expected this day to come. The wedding day created dreams of joyful expectation. No one is fully prepared, mentally or emotionally, for the day the dream turns into a nightmare and one is awakened into a far different reality.

The days and months following the finalization of a divorce are just as crucial. We need to remind ourselves that new challenges, as they always do, will tap into our feelings of vulnerability and inferiority. There will be periods of loneliness and despair. We may feel helpless and isolated in our thoughts and begin to question our self-worth. It is a time when we might be tempted by promises of a quick fix. Many make the mistake of jumping into other relationships in order to end the solitude and isolation. We have the need to feel worthwhile again. It is an appropriate need, but we must be careful that our needs do not overshadow common sense. All decisions, especially in terms of seeking a new relationship, should be made slowly and with a great deal of thought. The months following the divorce should be primarily a time for reflection.

We must not forget how our unhealthy solutions contributed to the infection and eroding of our marital relationships. By seeking another relationship right after one has ended, we are most likely underestimating the power of our neurotic goals. We must remember that these idealized goals act like drugs carrying all the promises of relief from pain. Of course we want to feel better about ourselves. Divorce challenges our feelings of self-worth and creates darkened thoughts of self-doubt. We want to be revived from the depths of despair that failure can bring and prove to ourselves and others that we are still worth loving. Without true reflection on the psychological lifestyle that brought us to this place, we raise the odds for more mistakes. It is here where we can be fooled by our ever-present neurotic solutions. If we ignore these realities in favor of simply feeling good, we are bound to repeat history.

Kelly's Story

Kelly and her husband Jack came to therapy with their relationship loosely held together. The tension between them had become a wall of anger and hate. Neither had the courage nor desire to self-reflect or to take ownership for their own mistakes. Each found it easier, and perhaps experienced a sense of power, to berate and accuse the other. They feared thinking of reconciliation, for taking personal responsibility might be interpreted as a weakness. Any small breath of life left in their marriage was smothered with hate and anger.

They were in serious financial trouble and steps away from bankruptcy. Their fighting had increased steadily in volume and intensity. After five months of counseling, both together and individually, they remained stuck in the blaming stage. Since neither took responsibility for their roles in the marriage, they saw divorce as the only solution. They separated with very little resolution.

During the last month of counseling with Kelly, she revealed she had been talking on the phone daily with someone she had met recently. She explained, "He is making me feel happy. I feel like a person for the first time in a long time. I think he really likes me. I look forward to his phone calls." I advised Kelly that it was not the right time to start a relationship, for three reasons:

First, Jack was still angry and upset and it would be foolish to do something that might add to his anger. Second, Kelly must think of her three young children and how it would affect them by bringing another man into the situation so soon. Third, Kelly was feeling lost and was fearful of her future. Getting attention from another man was a risky solution at best but seemed more like an act of desperation. Soon the man ended the phone conversations and Kelly expressed disappointment as she came down off her temporary emotional high.

A week had not gone by when Kelly announced she had met another man. They were both working for the same company and Kelly began sharing with him details of the state of her marriage. The man had been divorced for two years and knew that Kelly was soon to be available. Kelly explained, almost exactly as she had done with the previous short-lived relationship, "He shows me a lot of attention. He has been very helpful. He cares about me. It is so different from talking with Jack."

No amount of discussion could deter Kelly from continuing with the relationship or persuade her at least not to take it so seriously. She was once again living within her self-effacing solution, where receiving attention and admiration was all that mattered. Steeped in her neurotic solution, she was about to leave one relationship and move immediately to another. She was addicted to her need to be loved and wanted. In her selfish need to achieve self-worth in a neurotic way, the concerns for her children were secondary. The only way she might see the light was through the failure of the second relationship. If she married this man, it might take her second husband several years to tire of her constant need for reassurance. It might very well become another example of a long-term marriage that takes years to be recognized as neurotic. Kelly terminated therapy not wanting to hear any contradiction to her emotional striving. Two weeks later she filed for divorce from Jack.

Forgiveness

During the initial stages of reflection, one of the first tasks involves the issue of forgiveness. It entails not only the forgiveness of a former partner, but the need to forgive ourselves as well. As we begin the process of examining a marriage and our involvement in it, we might begin to see things about ourselves that are difficult to face. Seeing the way we spent years in neurotic ruts is upsetting and embarrassing.

Forgiving our partners is no easy task and many might balk at the thought of it. It is difficult enough to forgive ourselves. It forces us to face the many situations where we acted selfishly in trying to fulfill our neurotic needs. It is just as difficult to forgive our partners for also acting in self-serving manners. However, we need to realize that if we want to move on, forgiving ourselves and our partners is the first step. It is part of letting go.

The difficulty of forgiving is extremely well presented in the novel *The Shack*. The author, William Young, tells the story of a father who takes his two children on a camping trip. While at the camp, his daughter is brutally murdered by a stranger. The father, in the throes of depression, is invited to come to a shack and spend time with the Holy Trinity. In separate conversations with all three persons, he is presented with ideas that will eventually change his life. One particular conversation, however, he finds extremely difficult to accept: God asks him to forgive the murderer of his daughter.[14]

Initially I had a hard time even considering such a request.

Although I had accepted all the other ideas presented in the book with enthusiasm, the thought of forgiving such a sin seemed implausible. The father likewise struggles with such a consideration. God persists while the father keeps struggling with the request.

One evening I mentioned to a client my confusion regarding an aspect of forgiving. He thought for a few minutes and came up with an answer to how forgiveness is a possibility. He said, "If I follow the philosophy you have been teaching me, emotions are not something we can fully control, especially when they initially occur. It is expected for the father still to be angry. However, forgiveness is a cognitive process. It is a choice. It is something the father can choose to do."

I found my client's response to be enlightening. It might seem implausible to ask one partner to forgive the other, especially when there is still pain and hurt. The memories of the marriage recall when harsh and hurtful statements were made. With each reminder, they still ring loudly in each partner's mind. Each partner is likely to believe that the other partner's actions contributed to destroying a relationship and to tearing a family apart. Just as the father is perplexed and confused in Young's novel, each partner may be equally bewildered as to why they should forgive destructive and cruel behavior.

Once the marriage is over there is nothing we can do to change the past. We still might be experiencing the pain of divorce and might be driven to focus on the neurotic and selfish behavior of our partners. Wallowing in this state, however, certainly does more damage to our well-beings than it will ever do to our partners. Thomas Moore warns, "Blaming the other party for the ending of the relationship is understandable as a way of avoiding the pain caused by the inexorable, sometimes heartless demands of fate, but by avoiding that pain we may condemn ourselves to years of being haunted by the very emotions and images we are attempting to escape."[15] If we move away from all the personal insults and attacks, we might begin to see that our partners' behavior was not about us. With less emotion and more objectivity, we will come to see that our partners' behavior was more about where they were coming from. They had their unhealthy personal needs that had to be met. It was about them and not about us. The same could be said when we were attempting to fulfill our neurotic needs.

Using objectivity, we might begin to see that our relationships with our partners were relationships where people were unable to set themselves free of their neurotic needs and goals. It is no longer just one partner's responsibility. It is the task of each partner to take responsibility for the marital relationship. My client was right, I believe: we do have control over our thoughts and the conclusions we reach. Concentrating less on the emotions of rage and anger will free us to focus objectively on the new horizon before us.

Forgiveness goes beyond just letting our partners go. If we use this time of reflection well, we will undoubtedly find that we also were on neurotic paths. We are bound not to like many of the things we discover about ourselves. As we go through the process of forgiving our partners for their neurotic deeds, we must recognize the importance of forgiving ourselves for the times we were on our neurotic tracks. Just as it takes two to make a marriage loving and creative, it takes two to make it hateful and destructive. This is especially true for a marriage that goes on for years. Neither partner became unhealthy all of a sudden. It is more than likely the two people were connected by their neurotic systems for years.

As we discover our neurotic ways and the dynamics of our unhealthy approaches to life, forgiveness of ourselves and our partners must follow. The reflections on the marriage should never be about beating one partner down nor should it be one of self-torment. Reflection should be seen as a time to learn and grow. When speaking of a client in therapy and the time the client spends reflecting on his or her neurotic solution, Karen Horney explains where the client's focus needs to be:

> It is at bottom this question: does the patient want to keep whatever is left of the grandeur and glamour of his illusions, his claims, and his false pride or can he accept himself as a human being with all the general limitations this implies, and with his special difficulties but also for the possibility for growth?[16]

Divorce places each partner at a crossroad. It is time to make a choice. The recognition of having a neurotic solution is the first step in changing. Wisdom and common sense must replace our illusions of being more than human. Inferiority and anxiety are real; they are part of what it means to be human. It is foolish and naïve of us to think we can get beyond them. Marriages fail because one or both partners refuse to accept who they truly are. Marriages fail when one or both partners refuse to drop their defenses and choose to spend their time in protecting themselves from any hurt or pain. Love demands that we be true to ourselves as well as to others. By continuing to choose our neurotic solutions, we continue the lies to ourselves and to all those involved in our futures. Moving forward from the crossroad by forgiving ourselves for living without courage, we can now, with a new passion, move toward a new horizon.

Know Yourself

As difficult as it is to make the decision to divorce, it can offer an individual a wonderful and creative opportunity. If the proper effort is put forth, there is the possibility for a more meaningful and purposeful way of life. As this new stage of life begins, we need to remind ourselves that marriages end for a reason. As the years of marriage went on, we were more and more living within our unhealthy and neurotic solutions to life. By doing so, we were supporting an environment that lacked nourishment and love. It was a life of ongoing personal denial. We refused to admit to the terminal sickness of the relationship. Anxiety and the fear of change were dictating the choices we were making and pointing us in a defensive direction. It was a life of survival as opposed to one of growth and development. We remained stuck in a neurotic cycle that spun us nowhere.

Drained and exhausted, depressed and angry, we were fighting the inevitable. The environment of marriage had become stagnant, smothering any chance for a sense of self-worth or self-fulfillment. We were not aware of or perhaps denied the fact that we had choices. We could choose a healthy solution to life's challenges or we could choose to be unhealthy. We failed to see how both of our solutions, the healthy and the unhealthy, can function in a relationship. We failed to see, perhaps even from the beginning of the marriage, that in choosing a particular partner we might have made the choice from an unhealthy track. We presume, especially in the early years of marriage, that we chose our partners for admirable and healthy reasons. For some this might be so. In other marriages, without either partner knowing the basic dynamics and goals of his or her lifestyle, the unhealthy solution might be the main reason he or she married a particular person. A number of the stories we looked at showed this to be true. Anyone can be functioning with his or her neurotic solution and therefore will be unable to choose a marital partner for healthy reasons. Since our unhealthy solutions are filled with distortions and misguided perceptions, the choices we are making in this state become, at the very least, questionable.

Remaining unaware as the years of marriage continue on, we connect our unhealthy solutions to our partners' unhealthy solutions, which might turn into the primary part of our relationships. It may lie hidden beneath years of denial. As seen in the termination of long-term marriages, sooner or later the consequences of denial appear. It might be a deep financial debt as one partner tries to please the other. Depression might increase as one partner continues to live in a repressed environment. The children might move out of the home and leave two people who do not know each other anymore and have no idea of how to get along. Or, as happens in many marriages, the neurotic demands of one partner intensify to the point that the other partner can no longer bear it.

This final reason, perhaps the most common, leaves one partner no choice but to abandon the marital environment in order to regain a sense of the creative self and to begin living with a healthier solution. However, leaving the marriage does not guarantee mental health.

In the days and months following divorce, we need to remember why it was impossible for us to be healthy in an unhealthy environment. At the same time, however, we need to define how our personal approaches to life supported the inappropriate environments and unhealthy relationships in one way or another. It is our own personal cycles we want to focus on in order to define the way that we need to change. The last thing we want to do is to remain in a state of ignorance and then return to similar environments with the same neurotic solutions to life.

For perhaps the first time in our lives, based on the knowledge gained from the experiences of a poor relationship, this time of reflection allows us to fully face who we are and who we are not. Inferiority, our physical, mental and emotional limitations, must no longer be denied. Denial, both before and during the marital relationship, is what led to many of the tragic interactions in the marriage. Freeing ourselves from the prison of denial, we are capable, for the first time in a long time, to focus on our strengths and gifts.

As we reflect on our marital environments, we should also question if as children we were born into unhealthy environments. Perhaps members of our initial environments were too consumed with their own neurotic needs and therefore were unable to love and care for us in nourishing manners. As a result, we were unlikely to develop some of our gifts and talents. We were all born with a range of potential, but if these potentials were not fed and encouraged, they simply faded from existence or at best remained in infantile stages.

Being aware of the effects our initial environments had on us is incredibly important. As I tell my clients, we came from somewhere and that somewhere had tremendous influence on our development. Many environments do not enhance self-confidence and self-love. Many do the opposite. If we were born into a world of competition, one that was more self-serving than serving others or one that was oblivious to the notions of love and warmth, we were forced to go on the defensive and seek solutions to protect ourselves in order to survive. In survival mode, we lost genuine interest in others and began a life of self-service. We never developed the healthy attitude of "I-you-we" to the degree we needed to and had no choice but to center on protecting ourselves from further hurt and vulnerability.

For the sake of survival, depending on how limited our first environments were, we might have had to develop defensive approaches to life in order to guard our natural vulnerabilities. As we reach our adult lives, however, most of us are unaware we have developed these defensive solutions and that they now have become a way of life for us. Not having a clue as to whether we are healthy or not, we move on to adult challenges with the solutions we learned in childhood. Unless challenged to do otherwise, it is what we believe to be the right way. With the conviction that our solutions worked in our initial environments, we hold on to them, convinced this is what we need to do. When it comes to getting married, these solutions often walk up the aisle with us and remain in places of prominence throughout the marriage. In a very real sense, we repeat our childhood histories in terms of how we relate to others.

In recognizing the danger of remaining unaware of what we have become and why we chose to take on certain characteristics over others, the time for reflection following divorce gives us the opportunity to take a close look at the effects our initial environments had on us. It is not something that needs to be beaten to death nor is it a time to shirk responsibility by blaming others. The point is to learn the difference between healthy human strivings versus the ones that involve our own selfish need to protect ourselves. Our failure to do this previously is most assuredly what has led to numerous failures in marital relationships. It is more than likely that we, along with our partners, were functioning in one way or another with solutions intended to protect our vulnerabilities at all costs. With such thinking, as unconscious as it might have been, love and cooperation were not a priority.

Ryan's Story

Ryan was a middle child born between two sisters. As he grew older and became more aware of the environment in which he was living, he knew there was a great deal wrong with his family. For as long as he could remember, his parents slept in separate rooms and had very little communication between them. By the time he was a teenager, home was a place he did not want to be and he tried to be out of the house as much as possible.

Ryan's father was an alcoholic and the relationship between the two of them was nonexistent. All talking stopped between them when Ryan was about thirteen and continued that way for several years until his father died of alcohol-related symptoms. During the funeral, people approached Ryan asking how he was doing and how he was feeling. Ryan's pat response to all who asked was a simple "I'm fine." The main problem with this repeated response was that Ryan actually thought he was fine. With very little choice of doing otherwise during his developmental stages, repression had become an art form in Ryan's interaction with others and in dealing with his own internal emotions.

Ryan's mother was referred to by some of his friends as "the general." She was a harsh woman who lacked the ability to show any form of affection. There were never any words of warmth expressed between Ryan and his mother. During his high school years, this strange reality became more apparent to Ryan as he witnessed other parents and the relationships they had with their children.

Ryan had learned to deal with a life devoid of affection and trust. He began to go through life in a fog, with very few expectations or desires. Throughout college and after, he often felt uncomfortable with new situations, always feeling inadequate and unprepared. He never expressed these feelings to anyone, presuming, based on experience, that no one wanted to hear what he had to say.

Ryan entered his twenties unaware of the psychological effects of his childhood. Introspection and self-examination were never part of his day. He had learned to take life as it came and although he participated with others on a regular basis, he always was left with the feeling of being disconnected and alone. There were unidentified periods of depression, but they were ignored and considered commonplace. He basically went along with the flow, never realizing he had another choice.

Ryan's future wife, whomever she may be, will marry a person who expects very little in life, with few demands or wants. With an ego that barely had a chance to develop, Ryan will predictably be attracted to a woman who gives very little in terms of affection or concern for him. His marriage will most likely be all about her and have very little to do with him. He will not expect to receive joy or love from her and is prepared for a life of isolation and sacrifice. Without a great deal of introspection and perhaps the help of a therapist, the odds are very high that Ryan will eventually become part of the divorce statistics or remain in a marriage that has little life to it.

Following reflections on our childhood experiences and the experiences we had in our marriages, we then need to move our focus to the present. A great deal of thought needs to be given to defining the psychological lifestyles we have developed and how they still influence the choices we make. We must remember two principle notions regarding human development. First, we developed solutions to protect us from as many vulnerable and inferior feelings as possible. Second, the lifestyle characteristics we developed were done in a specific environment and were to serve a specific purpose. If the environment did not foster or nourish specific characteristics, such as seeing ourselves as potentially loving and creative, we then most likely entered adult life without them. As partners in marriage, we continue with the lifestyles with which we are most familiar. These two facts of life regarding our development demand a great deal of reflection.

Searching for our true selves by discovering our strengths and weaknesses should be one of our major tasks following divorce. Actually, we should be engrossed with it, most especially during this time of change and before new challenges arrive.

Reflection and the freedom to do so bring the opportunity to search for our talents and gifts and to begin to focus on the positive side of ourselves. Too often in our lives, especially in trying to keep a harmful marriage together, we are preoccupied more with survival than creativity. We make the tragic mistake of allowing fears, anxieties and the terror of failure to dictate our lives and influence all our decisions. It is the underlying factor and the cause for our spending years in unhealthy relationships. Becker calls for us to recognize two sides of our nature. He states, "The enemy of mankind is basic repression, the denial of throbbing physical life and the specter of death. The prophetic message is for the wholly unrepressed life, which would bring into birth a new man."[17] It might be nearly impossible to go through life without some repression. The fault, however, lies in the extent to which we tend to do it. This new unrepressed person Becker speaks of is the one who seeks to invent a new solution and a new approach to life. He or she seeks to relate to others, especially in intimacy, in an entirely different way. Following divorce and on the road to becoming a more complete person, this should be one of our primary goals.

Thomas's Story

Thomas was raised in a house where the family members were all strangers to one another. With no communication or sharing between them, Thomas learned to keep everything to himself and had almost no expectations of the people with whom he was romantically involved. He was active in many relationships but never felt truly part of his partners' lives. Repeating his childhood, he became an emotional loner among hundreds of strangers. He learned not to trust anyone with his fears, hurts and pain. He became convinced, based on his childhood experiences, that no one really cared. One of his early recollections represented his perceptions and expectations regarding relationships:

> I was about eight or nine years old. It was a beautiful summer day and I looked forward to playing army and basketball with my friends. I walked around the corner to the house of one of my friends and knocked on the side door. My friend came to the door and partially opened it. I was still excited about the day ahead until my friend announced he couldn't do anything that day. Just as he said these words, I heard the voice of another friend from inside. My friend then closed the door.
>
> I left the house and walked home crying. The rejection was extremely painful. Adding to the pain was the realization there was no one at home with whom to share this. I leaned on a tree and cried.

Unaware of the lifestyle he was developing, Thomas entered his adult years rating his life in the middle of a scale from one to ten. He explained to anyone who wanted to hear, "Sometimes life reaches a seven and those are really good days. Sometimes days drop to a two or three and you just have to work through it. Anyone who thinks life is a nine or ten has to be on something or is just plain naïve." It was only in his later years that he realized the resigned perceptions he had developed about life and relationships and the defensive solution that had become his belief system and mainstay. Entangled in a deep sense of inferiority and worthlessness, he was convinced life was just something to get through.

The lifestyle and solution he had developed far overshadowed his real human needs and wants. In graduate school, while training to be a social worker, Thomas took a psychological test along with the rest of his classmates. Based on the response to each question, the test rated the person from zero (the lowest) to nine (the highest) on specific areas of wants and needs. These areas of evaluation included how much the person needed inclusion and then rated how much the person actually sought to fulfill this need. It also rated how much the person needed warmth and affection and how much he or she actually sought it.

The psychology professor followed the test by dividing the class into groups of ten and directed each member to guess the score of the others and tell them why. All the students had been together for over three years, so they knew one another fairly well. When the attention turned to Thomas, each member of the group gave him a one or two. They were not critical in their feedback but felt that Thomas was extremely independent and did not need anyone for help or assistance.

Thomas scored nines in each area of the test. Thomas, as many individuals are, was a living contradiction. There was one side of himself he showed to others, his defensive and protective self, while his real self existed quietly within him. Buried silently within him were his real needs and desires. Thomas was not aware that he was living this contradiction and certainly not aware of it as he lived through years of marriage while raising five children. Having experienced very little joy or happiness during his childhood years, he unconsciously omitted these from his personal expectations. He believed strongly that others deserved joy and happiness, but for reasons he was convinced were correct, they were just not for him to experience. He worked hard to give his wife and children everything they wanted. Living way beyond their means, Thomas intended to fill their lives with everything they needed and more. Nearing his fortieth anniversary, his wife divorced him for not giving enough. She became Thomas's childhood friend closing the door.

Facing the realities of divorce, Thomas needed the ensuing months to be a time of deep reflection. In his attempts to get through his depression and anger, he needed first to forgive his wife for her behavior throughout most of the marriage. Only towards the last few years of his marriage did he realize that the relationship was all about pleasing her and fulfilling her needs. Next, as hard as it may be to admit, he needed to see how his solution to life actually enabled and fostered his wife's neurosis. In a sense, he was equally unhealthy. Finally, he needed to develop the courage to cease his unhealthy lifestyle and to learn to become vulnerable again. It would be the only way for him to achieve love for himself and to create an environment where he could be loved in return.

Love of Self and Others

Self-love is often overtaken and displaced by self-hate. To some, hate may be too strong a word. It is, however, at the very least, self-dislike. Neurosis is all about shame and dislike. The neuroses we choose, referred to as our unhealthy solutions, are developed for one simple reason: the refusal to accept ourselves for who we are. Even though we may accept the notion that no human being fully has what it takes to handle all the problems and challenges of life, we nonetheless often find this reality too overwhelming and too frightening to accept.

In the time of reflection following divorce, we need to recognize how unreasonable and detrimental it is to perceive ourselves with self-dislike. We spend a lifetime and certainly a great deal of time in our marriages pounding away at ourselves for being imperfect. We so easily miss the point that when we genuinely love another, we never expect that person to be perfect. So why, we should ask ourselves, do we expect perfection from ourselves? One of the goals in the time of reflection must include the awareness of the shameful, actually dishonorable, way we have been treating ourselves.

Along with our abilities, strengths and capacity for creativity and success, we also have limitations, are often helpless and certainly are capable of failure. All of us struggle for our entire lives with these two opposing attitudes about ourselves. When we refuse to accept this struggle, refuse to accept all forms of inferiority and feelings of self-doubt, we leave ourselves no choice but to do everything in our power to hide this reality from ourselves and others. It is with this mind-set—the need to avoid all imperfections—that we often enter into an intimate relationship with another. The more we feel the need to deny our humanness, the more the relationships with our spouses are founded on deceit and lies.

This denial of our humanness, fueled by our self-dislike, often becomes a primary part of many marriages.

There is often a fine line between having healthy goals versus neurotic strivings. The basic difference lies in whether or not we choose to accept our limitations and vulnerabilities. The neurotics ignore their limitations and strive for perfection, either through narcissism (control and dominance) or self-effacement (approval and acceptance). Through the use of either of these solutions, we demand that our spouses also ignore our imperfections and see us in an idealized manner. In doing so, we are demanding something that is impossible to achieve. We are making a marital connection that is bound to fail.

The person who chooses the healthy track recognizes his or her human limitations, yet places his or her focus on the possibilities of his or her strengths and abilities. It is only this type of person who is capable of a love relationship. This person has moved away from the selfish need to protect him or herself to a desire to share his or her complete self with another.

When we foolishly fall into the habit of comparing our actual selves to the idealized or perfect pictures for which we strive, we are left with feelings of dislike and even self-contempt for who we really are. In the process of making this comparison, any notion of self-love is overshadowed by self-contempt. The narcissist always wants more glory and fame and strives for it fearing his or her real self will show through. The self-effacing person never gets enough approval or confirmation and lives in fear that his or her basic inadequacy will be discovered.

When self-contempt is brought into a relationship by either partner, it becomes a formula for disaster. When we use our neurotic solutions as the primary basis for relating to our spouses, we are automatically creating walls between our partners and us. With the purpose of protecting ourselves from all that we dislike about ourselves, our responses to situations either become all about us or all about our partners. The narcissistic partner will demand admiration, control and dominance. The self-effacing partner will require approval, acceptance and admiration. Even when one partner does not use his unhealthy solution as his base, he is often drawn into the demands of the unhealthy partner, thus becoming unhealthy himself.

In either situation, we live in our own private worlds that exclude the genuine work of helping ourselves and our partners to be healthy. They are worlds that have a personal agenda: to protect ourselves from all threats from within and from without. In our selfish striving and the lack of courage to be our true selves, our intrinsic demands become a primary part of the relationship: "You can only see me as…" "You must always treat me as…" In reflection, we must recognize how we might have made such demands on our partners and our partners might have done the same to us.

Long-term marriages that are based on either partner's neurotic demands become long-term derisive ruts. In a non-nourishing environment, each partner, over years of marriage, perceives the other partner more and more only in terms of fulfilling his or her neurotic demands. The partner, more than any other person, becomes a target for his or her needs to be fulfilled and a means to reach his or her idealized image. When this takes place over a number of years, it is a sign that both partners are in their neurotic zones more often than not and are using each other to avoid the selves they fear being.

Many marital books describe this as codependency, which on one level may be true. It is, however, much deeper and more complicated than that. The neurotic demands are all-consuming and, over the years of marriage, begin to permeate the majority of marital interactions. In long-term marriages, individuals either become healthier or more neurotic. There is no such thing as the status quo. Couples either move in one direction or the other. When the relationship is mired in a neurotic system, it may take years to reach its final point of destruction. The failure at some point of long-term marriages must never be considered as sudden. When time is taken for reflection and the overall relationship is evaluated, it will be discovered how both partners did not participate in the relationship with their real selves.

The endless arguing, brutal fights and angry outbursts that take place over the duration of a conflicted marriage all have the self-centered demands of one or both partners as their starting points. The emotional eruptions that take place occur when one or both partners' demands are not met. When a client, married for a number of years, comes into therapy and begins to complain vehemently about her partner's behavior, she fails to realize that her complaints often say a great deal about her. It is not that she is responsible or to blame for her partner's behavior, but her complaints might very well be connected to her own neurotic system and her own desperate needs.

The narcissist will complain that his partner does not listen to him enough and rarely treats him as number one. He expects complete allegiance and his partner is never to disagree with his perspectives or beliefs. The self-effacing personality will complain she is never appreciated and is often taken for granted. She does not feel loved or wanted except to be of service to her partner. Neither realizes they are both connected by their neurotic solutions. Karen Horney explains, "What he does not feel is the fact that he responds to something which he himself has put into them."[18] In other words, each unhealthy partner has transferred his or her needs onto the other partner and often becomes dissatisfied, even enraged, when these needs are not met.

Mary Beth's Story

Mary Beth came to therapy in her forties. She explained she was presently involved in a relationship for the past three years with a divorced man. Lately she had been seeking more of a commitment from him with the hopes of getting married. She explained he was an alcoholic and drug abuser, but she felt the love and attention she showed him would cause him to change his ways. She also knew there were times when he was with other women, but he had recently promised to stop all other relationships. Each time he was drunk or high he apologized and expressed his deep love for her. She spent days being angry with him and then he in turn accused her of always being angry or in a bad mood. An emotional cycle, starting from the beginning of the relationship, kept repeating itself on a regular basis. Mary Beth often came to her therapy sessions angry and upset when any of these situations occurred.

Mary Beth was an intelligent person. She had a good job with a great deal of responsibility. However, even when she realized how illogical both her and her boyfriend's behavior was, she remained driven to make him change. When discussion turned to her background, she explained she came from a family of four children and, as the youngest, she took care of her mother. Her father died when she was young and her mother became involved in a relationship with a man whom she claimed to love. Mary Beth explained:

> The only time she was happy was when she was with him. He disappointed her most of the time and didn't show up for weeks at a time. My mother then spent hours lying on the couch in the dark, which made me feel horrible for her. I spent a great deal of time trying to make her happy. I could never get her to see this man as less important than my sisters and me. I was trying to find out if she loved me.

Mary Beth also talked about her marriage of twenty-two years. She explained, "After a few years of marriage, he became emotionally and sometimes physically abusive. He worked long hours and was rarely around for the children and me. We fought a great deal and I could never get him to respect me. I never felt he really loved me. Each time I confronted him about his behavior, he blamed me by putting me down in any way he could. Our divorce was ugly and very expensive."

Mary Beth could not make the connection between the relationships with her mother, her former husband and her present boyfriend. Even when she did see herself as the common denominator, she remained more focused on them rather than the role she played in her relationships with them. Beginning with her childhood experiences, Mary Beth was left with the feeling of abandonment and insignificance. Her mother spent years in depression and was only happy when her boyfriend came around. Having been rejected by her mother for years, Mary Beth could not deal with the pain of being ignored and did everything she could to win her mother's affection. This striving to prove she was lovable through the eyes of another became her neurotic addiction.

She continued this drive into her adult years, the only difference being the target of her need to achieve her goals.

Mary Beth's lifestyle was established in reaction to her childhood experiences. She never resolved the unhealthy lifestyle she developed and therefore brought her psychological solutions into significant relationships she had as an adult. The feelings of being insignificant and unwanted were dictating the choices she made. In order to be in the process of conquering these feelings, she required a worthy target in a specific type of partner. It had to be a relationship where she had to beg and fight for attention. In her neurotic solution to life, both her former husband and present boyfriend were perfect targets for her to act out her unhealthy striving. Both of them, based on their unhealthy lifestyles, were not about to show her consistent love. Their behavior tapped into Mary Beth's greatest fears and was followed by her obsessive drive to make a connection with them.

For Mary Beth ever to have a chance to be healthy, she needed to come to terms with her own self-hate. She needed to learn how the self-hate originated and grew out of her initial environment and how her solution was created as a response to these experiences. Finally, she needed to be able to define and recognize the characteristics and dynamics of her neurotic solution and hopefully at some point learn how destructive she was being to herself, both in and out of these relationships.

This is the task every human being must perform. For those who do not perform this examination there is a high risk of repeating the cycle they originally created and bringing it into every area of their adult lives. In order to overcome the vicious cycles of which we are capable, the perceptions we have of ourselves, especially self-hate, require redefining. There must be a reexamination of the solutions we developed as a result of these self-perceptions. A marriage that is permeated by distorted self-perceptions and unhealthy solutions is bound to be a marriage that is troubled. As the longevity of Mary Beth's persistent neurotic solution reveals, it becomes more understandable how one or both partners can exist within their neurotic solutions in both short and long-term marriages.

We bring our healthy and unhealthy solutions into our marriages. It is impossible for any of us to be perfectly healthy, which means we fall into our neurotic tracks at one time or another. In many marriages, unfortunately, the neurotic solution is the primary part of the relationship with a spouse. It is during these times in the marriage when the partner is acting out his or her neurotic needs and using a spouse to reach his or her idealized goals. The expectations any of us place on our partners to relieve us of our pain and to make us feel good about ourselves create tasks our partners can never consistently fulfill and certainly not fulfill completely. The expectations, over years of marriage, turn into rigid demands and intensify. Anger and rage soon follow whenever these demands are not met. Distance is created between the partners and the marriage takes on a downward slope.

In many marriages the conflict between each partner's lifestyle can go on for years. It is most likely not evident to outsiders, for it is often hidden behind the closed doors of the marriage. Most couples put on the so-called good show for friends to see, but when spouses are on their own either partner may return to his or her redundant battle for self-esteem and self-worth. The partner once again becomes the target for the achievement of the other partner's neurotic striving to be perfect. As witnessed by Mary Beth's experience with relationships, self-love can never be reached when one is struggling with and is tormented by feelings of inferiority. Self-love cannot function if it is continuously interrupted by the neurotic need to overcome all vulnerability and self-hate.

If Mary Beth truly loved herself, she would have realized how unhealthy the demands were of those with whom she was connected. Staying with her neurotic solution enabled the others to continue relating to her with their neurotic demands. She could not expect to change them, but by treating herself with more respect she would have been in the position to move on and stop the neurotic bond.

Numerous people, perhaps unaware, enter marriage without genuine self-love. Many, in fact, use the marital platform as a means to achieve at least some level of feeling worthwhile and to overcome the many negative feelings they have about themselves. This never works for the simple reason that our partners are actually incapable of making us love ourselves. Love for self must always come from within. It is only then that partners can confirm this love by the way they respond with love.

When one or both partners enter a marriage with a lack of self-worth, they enter it with an ingrained conviction of being unlovable in some way. As a result, they can never trust the love they may receive.

As we've seen, there are basic reasons for the success of marriages and for the demise of marriages. From the perspective of a concrete philosophy and numerous illustrations, we can conclude that marriages start with the individual first. Healthy individuals with healthy approaches to life develop and maintain healthy relationships. When one or both partners fall into their neurotic solutions, the relationship ceases being productive and genuine love is put to the side. Having taken the mystery out of why some relationships work and others do not, partners in relationships are destined for one of three outcomes:

The first outcome originates from the position of both partners' willingness to accept each other and themselves for who they truly are. It starts with the realization by both partners that they will experience anxiety and fears and often feel inferior in response to various challenges. They accept that their partners will often feel the same. Both partners are not afraid to recognize when these fears and anxieties are allowed to dictate their solutions to challenges. They are watchful for when, where and how they are capable of being unhealthy. From the position of love and patience, both know their partners are capable of the same.

A marital relationship, by definition, is loving and creative when both partners know their vulnerabilities and are willing to share them with their partners. It is when both partners know the difference between their neurotic and healthy solutions and know their partners' solutions as well. It is when two people, out of concern and compassion for each other, help each other out of their unhealthy tracks when these times occur and encourage self-love with genuine love for each other.

The second outcome involves one partner who comes to the realization that the relationship is becoming more unhealthy and destructive to both partners as individuals. It is a time when the other partner is blind to his or her neurosis and refuses all forms of self-reflection or help from outside sources. As the marriage continues on in months and years, each partner's perceptions and goals become polar opposites. It is a time when one partner fully realizes the disconnection between the two of them.

The partner reaching this realization may not be able to end the relationship at this time for one reason or another. It is imperative for this partner to search for the ways and means to remain as healthy as possible. This partner needs to see there is more to his or her life than the relationship with his or her partner. There are children, a career and a social life. Most especially the partner has him or herself. As difficult as it may seem in an unhealthy marriage, with faith and courage the partner with this realization needs to find the strength to move forward with meaning and purpose.

The third outcome becomes a necessity when the first and second options are no longer possibilities. It is a time when one or both partners cannot let go of their neurotic solutions. It is a time when the love between them has ceased and is replaced with resentment and discontent. One or both partners reach the full realization they cannot be real while remaining in this environment. Acceptance, forgiveness and courage are necessary. It is time to search for a new horizon.

Part Four

Creating a Successful Marriage

Now let's turn to the factors that are common to healthy and creative marriages. We'll discuss how to keep a marriage healthy and how each partner can assist the other in staying on a healthy track.

Correcting the Neurotic Connection

We have presented one definition of a healthy individual as a person who knows his or her neurosis and makes the decision not to live off it. The same concept can be applied to the definition of a healthy marriage. A healthy marriage is one where both partners are aware of their neurotic paths and how they may be neurotically connected. With this awareness, they are able to assist each other not to live off this connection when responding to each other or in dealing with a life problem.

In order to achieve a healthy marriage, both partners must be willing to see the possibility of being a match to the other partner's neurotic track. This is especially mandatory when the marriage has already fallen into a primarily neurotic connection and has been operating that way for some time. To correct this debilitating connection, both partners must be open to seeing the possibility when and under what circumstances they are on their own neurotic tracks.

When one partner's reaction to a situation is obviously unhealthy in a marriage, it does not necessarily mean the other partner is free from fault. One may be more obvious, but it is more than likely the other partner is supporting the first partner's unhealthy solution with a neurosis of his or her own.

Shaun and Heather's Story

In Shaun and Heather's marriage, Shaun was often angry. His outbursts and need to dominate a situation were rarely questioned, because Heather suffered from a severely low opinion of herself and lived in fear of losing her husband and being on her own. She had a tremendous need for acceptance and Shaun was the primary target of fulfilling this need. It was nothing short of an addiction. She craved a so-called "fix" on a regular basis and her husband was the drug of choice. Confronting him was out of the question. Heather rarely risked expressing her personal opinions because of the way she felt about herself and her fear of losing Shaun. Even though she had abilities and talents, her self-effacing solution acted as a lid on her positive feelings and insights. She needed to be accepted so desperately that she relied on Shaun's acceptance no matter what the price.

Directly and indirectly, both were often tapped by each other's manner of behavior. She was often tapped by Shaun's anger and she interpreted the anger as rejection, thus moving her neurotically to try again to get his approval. Shaun, on the other hand, saw her as weak and only approved of her when she agreed with him. As a direct result of their personal solutions to counteract human inferiority—narcissism and self-effacement—they were more connected to each other's neurotic and defensive solutions than their healthy tracks.

As we've seen in neurotic marriages, both partners in the marriage spend a great deal of time tapping into each other's feelings of inferiority and vulnerability. When these times do occur, it is as if one partner is agitating his or her spouse's open wound (the spouse's fears and vulnerabilities). The purpose of doing so, even though it is the antithesis of a love relationship, is to control the spouse and try to minimize the number of times the first partner is liable to feel inferior. Adler recognizes the possibility for having a neurotic connection by explaining how couples often enter marriage with inappropriate aims and continue with these emotional demands throughout the marriage. He explains, "Some people marry for economic security; they marry because they pity someone; or they marry to secure a servant."[1] In most cases, neither partner is actually fully aware of his or her underlying psychological motivations. Nonetheless, the defense of personal inadequacy with a neurotic solution often does take place in a marriage and is always destructive to the relationship.

For a marriage to have the possibility of being healthy, it is the responsibility of each partner to become aware of the numerous occasions when neurotic interactions with his or her partner are a possibility. Without this awareness, both partners are more than likely, out of ignorance, to fall into their neurotic tracks on a regular basis. Awareness will also help one partner not to react automatically to the times the other partner is responding in an unhealthy way. Without knowing the difference between their neurotic versus healthy solutions, both partners will lose the opportunity of being able to evaluate how they are connected to each other in problem solving. They will also lose the opportunity to learn how they both might enable each other's unhealthy approach to life. As Adler explains, "The attitude of every individual toward marriage is one of the expressions of his life style: we can understand it if we understand the whole individual."[2] It is here where Adler emphasizes the need for each partner to see the other as a whole person, meaning one with talents and flaws. This is not a negative exercise but the first step in making the relationship healthy.

Without this understanding of who they are and who they potentially can choose to become, both partners can easily fall into the pattern of reinforcing their neurotic connections. Even when achieving neurotic goals, they are losing the larger challenge of having a healthy relationship and therefore they are eroding the relationship in the long run. Not being aware of their neurotic connection is a primary reason why so many marriages function under the cloud of sadness and anger. Over time, especially in marriages longer than twenty-five years, the relationship turns into an ongoing and redundant struggle. It then reaches the point where the spouses do not want to spend time together and prefer the times they are apart. In an increasing amount of cases, one or both partners choose to make this separation permanent.

A good way to avoid the neurotic connection, besides the emphasis on awareness, is to stop treating each interaction in isolation. Rather than looking at a response from a partner in isolation, each partner should ask the primary question: Is this coming from my partner's healthy track or unhealthy track? As Adler suggests, it helps a great deal when spouses look for the common denominator in a particular situation and view the incident as being part of the whole.

A key hint to when one's partner has been tapped is when the partner's response does not logically seem to fit the solution to a problem being addressed. For example, if the partner's response of anger seems like an overreaction to the situation, it is likely that he or she has been tapped. Or perhaps one partner is overly upset or hurt by a situation in a way that exceeds what actually took place. When one partner reacts in either of these ways, it is not uncommon for the other spouse to react automatically to the illogical statement. Rather than trying to understand the underlying reasons for the illogical response to a situation, most spouses fall into the trap of responding directly to the illogical behavior or statement.

This type of scenario happens in all marriages, even the best of them. We have all fallen into this trap. Once this happens and the conversation continues, both partners now react to each other's illogical statements. We have, perhaps due to a lack of understanding, demeaned our partners for their attitudes. Then our partners, feeling slighted, respond to being put down. To avoid or stop this destructive line of communication, at least one partner needs to observe that the statements are illogical, not react impulsively and understand something else is going on. Many times the "something else" is that the other partner is reacting to being tapped and feeling vulnerable.

Illogical content always comes from the neurotic track. The partner's perspective on the incident taking place is distorted by personal fears and vulnerabilities. When illogical statements by a partner are made, one can presume that the partner's vulnerability has been tapped and his or her statement or behavior comes from his or her reaction to feeling vulnerable. The other partner can be helpful, as opposed to adding to the turmoil, by responding to the underlying reasons for the original statement rather than adding to the tension. By understanding how the lifestyle functions in all of us, partners can reach beneath behavior or statements and respond to the inferiority through reassurance and love. By addressing the underlying origin of the behavior or statement, spouses can help their partners not to let inferiority dictate their behavior and free them to make a healthier choice.

Marty and Nicole's Story

During Marty and Nicole's first therapy session, the spouses were in the middle of a conflict. The couple had hosted a party over the weekend that included people from Nicole's workplace. Nicole's guests were people from the so-called fast lane who not only were making tons of money, but also made sure people knew of their success. They were the type who expressed themselves with a superior attitude and looked down at the so-called "have nots."

Nicole's guests at the party intimidated Marty. He was from a very different background and was in a far different career situation. All the talk of money, success and the luxuries and power such people wielded affected him tremendously. Marty was either not fully aware of how inferior he felt or did not want to admit it. As the evening went on, he became overwhelmed with the conversations taking place and began displacing his inferiority feelings. Marty's feelings of inadequacy were ignited and his anger grew. When Bob, a guest at the party, said something inappropriate, Marty sensed the opportunity to be superior and to counteract his inferior feeling. Marty made a very degrading and biting statement to Bob. Putdowns and a quick tongue were common defense tactics used by Marty when he felt inferior. Silence and stares followed.

Nicole overheard the belittling statement made to Bob. She was both embarrassed and enraged. Nicole brought the conversation back to money and success. Once the guests departed, Marty and Nicole fought about what had happened.

The fact that Nicole was angry with her husband's retort was understandable. Her husband's remarks were out of place. However, rather than trying to understand why the situation occurred, she reacted to her own embarrassment and how she was affected.

It is at this common point where most couples make a crucial mistake. It would have been more helpful if Nicole had not immediately reacted. Nothing was to be accomplished with her anger. Sensing her displeasure and anger, Marty reacted to Nicole's comments defensively and then she responded to his and so on.

Even though it takes a great deal of patience, it would have been psychologically healthier if Nicole paused a moment to recognize Marty's statement as being inappropriate and out of place but dictated by his own feelings. By understanding the concepts of lifestyle and the defensive solutions that exist in us all, Nicole would have realized her husband's caustic statement was a sign he was tapped and felt vulnerable and inferior. It certainly was not the first time she witnessed him act this way.

With insight and sensitivity toward her husband, she could have realized that her guests at the party made her husband uncomfortable. By objectively understanding the nature of human vulnerability, especially when it occurred in her partner, Nicole could have been more aware, either before or during the party, that her husband would be intimidated by some of the people. He might dislike what they represented. If she was more sensitive to these human factors, especially his feelings of inferiority, the nonsensical battle that ensued may have never reached the heights it did.

Situations like Marty and Nicole's often take place in marriages. They start out small and then escalate to something bigger. The most unfortunate thing about these skirmishes is they can be avoided. A common reason for many fights in a marriage is that spouses do not take the time to understand each other, most especially in how and when they feel vulnerable and inferior.

Most marital disagreements reach levels of ongoing conflict when partners are not working at the marriage from a lifestyle—the partners' inferiority feelings and neurotic solutions—perspective. Those who do use these concepts know both partners have vulnerabilities, have fears and experience feelings of inferiority. As partners, they also know each of them has defensive solutions to these feelings. All relationships, along with having fun and happy times, require this type of awareness. Knowledge about each other will lead to insight and create the possibility for mutual growth. If either partner refuses to do the work, the marriage will experience continuous conflict and may eventually fail. If either partner does not take the time to understand the other in terms of neurotic solutions, the relationship will continuously waste time and effort in useless conflicts. It is so much more satisfying to learn to understand and fulfill each other.

Helping Each Other To Be Healthy

Marty and Nicole's story shows how a lack of understanding can easily turn into a crisis. It is not unusual for anyone to use his or her neurotic solution at a moment's notice. Because of the daily events of life, especially those unique to a marriage, both partners can easily make the mistake of allowing outside variables to affect and run their lives. A neurotic rut is nothing more than a person's way of handling feelings of inferiority.

When a neurotic reaction occurs with one partner, the other partner has the opportunity to play a constructive role in the relationship. With caring and insight, a partner can be ready to recognize when and how the other partner uses his or her neurotic solution and see it for what it is. It is not about the first partner but more about what is going on with the other partner. It is a time when the first partner has the opportunity and is called to help his or her partner return to a healthy track. To punish him or her for choosing a neurotic solution is always ineffective and always damaging to the marriage.

Genuine love and caring can help a partner out of a neurotic rut and offer an environment that allows the partner to drop his or her defenses. In addition to full and genuine caring, it takes understanding of the partner's lifestyle and how it is used to protect inferiority. In other words, love must also come with insight. Love is important, but equally important is the understanding of each other psychologically.

When each partner gets into the habit of thinking of lifestyle, it can even help prevent the partners from falling into this trap in the first place. The absence of this kind of love—caring with insight—is often a tragic omission in many marriages. I often ask married clients how they are helping their spouses to be healthy or how they nourish their partners. Most spouses admit they never thought of marriage in this way: as a relationship that is responsible for nurturing the other person. Once learned and applied, however, they reap the benefits almost immediately.

Tracy and Bruce's Story

Married for over twenty years, Tracy and Bruce could hardly look at each other when they first came for counseling. In fact, they had not looked into each other's eyes in a very long time. Both were angry, hurt and depressed. As each of them related their versions of the problem, it became obvious both were overwhelmed and exhausted. During the past few years, it seemed there was never enough money to pay even the basic bills on time. The situation was a tremendous drain on both of them. Tracy and Bruce were both being tapped and feeling powerless about their abilities to cope. Silently, each was ashamed to admit he or she felt like a failure.

Both Bruce and Tracy tried to deal with the day-to-day money issues on their own rather than with each other. Their individual approaches included wishing the problem would simply just go away. They both needed a break from feeling so overwhelmed. When they were together, each became a constant reminder to the other of how bad the situation was. Friends or even strangers were easier to be with, since they were unaware of the problem and therefore did not tap them as they did each other. The lack of money became a constant source of irritation between them. Their feelings of being helpless eventually turned into an anger that they focused on each other.

When they were going through therapy, I asked both spouses questions requiring openness. The goal of therapy was to encourage them to express honestly how they personally felt about the money issues, especially with no solution in sight. The process toward honesty involved peeling away one thought or emotion after another in order to reach their true feelings. As with most of us, the more honest feelings lay beneath layers of defenses and rationalizations.

With time and encouragement, Tracy and Bruce began to put their defensive anger aside and talk about their feelings. Bruce expressed that he felt like a failure and like he was letting everyone down. He always presumed he could take care of his family and the present situation made him ashamed and embarrassed. As he spoke, a real turning point occurred. With tears in his eyes, he turned to his wife and said, "I am so sorry for being a failure."

For the first time in a very long time, Bruce spoke from deep within himself and without an attacking defensive wall. His wife was surprised, but she immediately responded with compassion. She told him it was never his fault and they would find a way to work it out.

When it came time for Tracy to peel away her defensive layers, she was able to admit she too was terrified of the situation and was looking for someone to blame. She was now able to see that the person she was blaming was her husband, which only increased the mountain of anger between them. Tracy admitted she was disappointed in her husband for not making more money and that she had made him totally responsible for the situation. Even though she was part of the problem, until now she was taking no responsibility for the financial situation.

With this new type of honesty initiated by Tracy and Bruce, the two were able to start the process of becoming a couple again. They could now face the challenge together rather than acting against each other. Realizing both were being tapped by money issues, they could empathize with each other's feelings of vulnerability. They could move from being totally subjective to a more objective perspective, thus coming up with a better game plan for their financial situation.

The most important accomplishment related to this marital problem was that they both were able to work through their neurotic defensive anger. By letting down their defensive shields, they could begin the process of revealing to each other personal feelings of fear and inferiority.

While in therapy, both Bruce and Tracy came to realize they never had a psychological philosophy about marriage, nor did they have a philosophical base to utilize when dealing with their problems. Without an understanding of their own vulnerabilities, feelings and constitution, neither of them knew where to start when a problem arose. Experiencing the results of being more open, they could see how much more could be accomplished by understanding the dynamics of lifestyle as it applied to their marriage and to their specific problem with money. Couples who do not take the time to reach mutual understanding of each other often spend years reacting to the other partner's emotional reactions. More and more distance between the two of them occurs while animosity builds. When spouses are in therapy and are arguing, I often ask them to hold hands. It is a good gesture, especially when the fire between the spouses begins to burn. Anger and arguing creates distance, something that is hard to have when you are holding hands.

Dealing with Crisis

Marriage is a learning process about who we are and who our partners are. A crisis in a marriage, rather than being destructive, can be an opportunity for growing together. Most clients come into therapy in the middle of some sort of crisis and sometimes it is major. A crisis is handled poorly, because both partners are ignoring a neurotic connection that was part of their relationship for some time. The neurotic connection, unknown to them, was creating consequences that were interfering with having a loving relationship. Rather than learning and growing with each other, many couples spend more time and put more energy into protecting their own fears and vulnerabilities. As a result, they often end up growing distant and waiting for the next conflict. Living on a neurotic track and relating to a partner through this solution will eventually lead to a marital crisis, as we'll see with Richard and Claudia.

Richard and Claudia's Story

In Richard's first session with me he immediately related that his wife had discovered he was having an affair. The affair had been going on for a number of months and he confessed confusion as to what he wanted to do. He was enjoying the outside relationship but was feeling tremendous remorse about hurting his wife. There were problems in the marriage prior to the affair, but it had never reached this crisis level before.

Claudia, his wife, came to therapy the next day and was obviously distraught. She was hurt and angry. She spoke about divorce and how she wanted revenge. She was feeling extremely vulnerable about her future.

I asked Claudia if there was any possibility that she would give her husband a chance to rectify his behavior. I explained to her that affairs do not happen in isolation and there are reasons they take place. As difficult such behavior is to accept, I further explained there were underlying factors why Richard chose such a solution at this time in his life. As she listened to the concepts of lifestyle and that a marriage entails both healthy and unhealthy connections, she began to see the crisis from another point of view. She was willing to take the time to discover why the affair happened and to examine it in a wider context. Although our ensuing conversations in therapy were troubling and painful to her, they were productive.

As we discussed their marital relationship in our sessions together, the couple realized the marriage had grown distant over the years. They had grown accustomed to the usual family interruptions and responded mainly to family situations rather than each other. Now their three children had grown up and were on their own. It had been a long time since the spouses had interacted with each other on a personal level.

This type of marital scenario is not uncommon in many marriages. The raising of our children, our career responsibilities, dealing with financial issues and numerous other real life concerns often take away from not only nurturing ourselves, but also nurturing the marital relationship.

Claudia and Richard had developed personal idiosyncrasies and particular patterns of behavior as the years passed. They were not aware that some of their behavior was damaging to the marriage and was creating distance between them. However, during the first stage of therapy, neither wanted to take responsibility for what was happening over the years of marriage. In the isolated worlds each had created for him or herself, neither took the time to think about what was going on in the mind and heart of the partner. The basic elements of marriage—communication, sharing and spending time together—were rarities in their marriage. Both of them were ignoring the harmful consequences of the choices they were making. Eventually, they became enablers and supporters of each other's mistaken lifestyle, never questioning the direction the relationship was taking.

As more pieces of their marital puzzle came together, it revealed a husband who often worked very late, using his career to fill the void in his life. Claudia had become very involved in town politics, causing her also to be out many evenings. When they were home together, they ate while watching television and then later in the evening watched programs in separate rooms. Richard usually fell asleep watching a ball game and did not go to bed until late at night. On most mornings he left for work before Claudia awoke.

As Claudia and Richard described the daily routines of their lives, I asked if they ever thought where the marriage was heading. Did they ever wonder what was going on with the other spouse? They realized that neither of them was actually participating in the marriage, but they were responding to their own needs, whatever they seemed to be. There was very little meaningful interaction between them and the distance had grown greater and greater. Both sensed it from time to time but were afraid to question their relationship or do anything about it.

With the insights they were getting from therapy, they began to see their marriage had been a crisis waiting to happen. After they experienced the devastating consequences of Richard's affair, therapy became a tremendous challenge to explore the possibilities for saving their marriage. As each addressed and came to terms with his or her individual lifestyle and realized the effects each of their defense systems had on the marriage, they started to take personal responsibility for the present crisis in their marriage. To revive a marriage, this is always a mandatory step: mutual responsibility.

Claudia and Richard were good people lost in their own personal mazes. Claudia, based on her self-perception, expected little from the marriage from the very beginning. She had very low self-esteem and never expected to be fully loved. She handled housewife duties and was a good mother. Yet, due to her lack of self-love, she was hesitant to be a complete partner.

Richard was aware of his wife's shyness and the low opinion she had of herself. Throughout the years of marriage, he never considered his role as husband and the way he passively supported her self-image and approach to life. He never put himself in a position to help her grow and perhaps help her with her self-perception.

Richard came from a very provincial background. He was an only child sent to a boarding school at thirteen. Growing up, he was surrounded with superficial relationships. He grew accustomed to being alone and surviving on his own. He knew little about a loving relationship.

In therapy, rather than just focusing on the crisis created by the affair, Richard and Claudia looked at their relationship from a lifestyle point of view. They learned that all couples bring healthy and unhealthy solutions into their marriages. Once Richard and Claudia were able to recognize and admit to both their healthy and unhealthy approaches to life, they began to see how each of their neurotic tracks was destructive to the marriage. By allowing feelings of personal inferiority to dictate their behavior, they saw how they forgot each other's needs. This omission led to an erosion of their relationship and opened the door to further unhealthy behavior.

There are marital cases that do not reach this level of crisis. Yet, as with this couple, many do not see the possibilities for a crisis and how it can occur at any time. Some marriages set the stage for an affair by one partner. Understandably, no couple ever really wants to consider this possibility. However, if each person in the marriage does not try to understand the other fully and shows very little concern for the partner's feelings, then there usually is someone else who will. People seek nourishment from other people and want to feel good, even if it is from an inappropriate source. Each person in a marriage should be unafraid but aware of this possibility and wise enough to do all he or she can to keep it from happening.

The final blow for Richard and Claudia was the affair. As we moved on in our therapy sessions, I asked Richard if he ever considered how his wife felt at this point in their marriage. Was she lonely when he kept coming home so late? Did she miss the children being around? Did he ever think she might need to talk to him during dinner? How did she feel going to bed alone every night? Richard admitted to ignoring that something was wrong with their relationship, but he lacked the knowledge and courage to do anything about it. It was easier to ignore the problems. Their marriage became one of day-to-day survival.

I asked Claudia similar questions. I asked her not just to focus on the affair and the crisis it had caused but to consider her responsibility for allowing the marriage to reach the point it did. With a great deal of reflection and honesty, they both came to realize they had fallen into their own neurotic shells. They had allowed the marriage to erode and decay.

With time and a great deal of courageous work, both Richard and Claudia were able to forgive each other for the way each had behaved in the marriage. They were able to take more responsibility for the choices they had made and how they ignored the consequences of these choices. They learned and accepted the importance of knowing not only their own fears and vulnerabilities, but also how mandatory it was for them to be aware of a spouse's sensitivities and needs. Richard and Claudia learned how important it was for each of them to begin sharing who they truly were, emphasizing all their feelings, thoughts and needs.

With this new knowledge, Richard and Claudia were able to assist each other not only to choose a healthier solution, but also to get on the healthier track that makes love possible. The affair was still difficult for both to deal with, but now they had the resources to see the crisis in a new light and understand the unhealthy marital solution they had been supporting. With effort and caring, they both had the possibility to reconnect.

Sharing Vulnerabilities and Fears

Another mandatory component to having a successful marriage is mutual acceptance and understanding of each other as human beings. Anyone can love a person's strong points. It is also easier to be honest with a spouse, or anyone else, about personal things we like about ourselves or in which we have confidence. However, when it comes time to be fully open and include areas of vulnerability or things that make us feel small and fearful, sharing becomes more difficult.

For true, lasting and complete success in a marriage, each person must be able to trust his or her partner with all, not part of, his or her human feelings, most especially those that make the partner feel vulnerable. Each needs to be able to talk about when he or she is being tapped and how he or she actually feels when a problem occurs. A key component of a healthy marriage is to help each other with feelings of vulnerability and assist each other in making the healthy choice.

As we discussed earlier in the story of Ron and Susan, Susan knew of her husband's fear of tension and his exaggerated need for peace. With this awareness, she had the opportunity to help him avoid falling into his neurotic solution by demanding total peace and no tension in order not to be tapped. When there were times Ron did choose his neurotic solution, Susan had more understanding about why he was behaving the way he was rather than simply reacting to it or demeaning him.

Jay's Story

Jay initiated therapy following a crisis he had with his sixteen-year-old son, Chris. Jay was noticeably upset over the incident and extremely sorry that it had happened, explaining:

> Chris and I got into a huge shoving match one night and actually took swings at each other. I had picked Chris up early from a party. I know he was embarrassed that I came to get him, but drinking was taking place at the party and I wanted him to be

no part of it. There was a lot of yelling on the way home and when we arrived home it became physical. I hate myself for it, but I live in fear for my children and how they might get seriously hurt by what's going on in our society. It's driving me crazy with worry.

Jay, sincerely upset, admitted to having a temper. This was not the first time he had exploded in this manner. During the early years of his marriage, he said, there were times he pushed his wife. He expanded on his relationship with his wife:

My wife, Lauren, is right about the fact that I have a temper. It was wrong what I did early in the marriage, but it hasn't happened in twenty years. My son, Chris, is sixteen and my daughter, Sarah, is fifteen. I love them so much, but I know what is out there. The drugs and drinking are out of control. That's why I picked Chris up the other night.

When it comes to the children, my wife and I are on different pages. Lauren is much more liberal than I am. She doesn't have the same worries I do. Lauren grew up differently and had a nicer childhood. I was no saint and I know more about the bad things in life than she does. She sometimes thinks I am crazy and that I am too hard on the kids. She even threatens to leave me.

Jay's concerns for his children were legitimate. He was involved in a common conflict that many parents have with their children. His out-of-control temper was another factor with which Jay agreed. There was definitely the issue of underage drinking and Jay admittedly allowed his emotions to get out of hand. As importantly, this recent incident created a marital crisis. His wife, Lauren, came alone for a session to present her side of the story. She explained:

Jay is a wonderful person, but he has always had a temper. It involved us at one time but not any longer. Now it's involving the children and I have to protect them. This week's incident can never happen again.

I know Jay is worried about our two children. I think he worries too much. Maybe I don't worry enough. But I think they are good kids and I trust them. Maybe that is foolish but I still think Jay is too hard on them.

Neither Jay nor Lauren was totally right or totally wrong. They were being challenged with a parenting situation and they differed in perspective and approach. Lauren was fully aware of Jay's fears when it came to the children but admitted that they did not discuss their perspectives and feelings enough. Emphasis was placed more on each of their reactions to the children and it was turning into a point of contention between the two of them. Because Jay was so open about his fears and admitted they might be exaggerated, it was a good time for him and Lauren to sit down and talk about what was important. They already respected each other's fears and vulnerabilities, but these items needed to be discussed more openly. Finally, a mutual game plan needed to be established so the spouses could approach parenting together while respecting each other's thoughts and feelings.

Defining Love

By emphasizing the psychological connections we have in relationships, it does not mean the importance of love is dismissed or is considered secondary when it comes to having a successful marriage. Love, in contrast to being secondary, is very much a part of the concepts we're discussing. In order to understand how this is so, love needs a definition.

There are many definitions of love and many ways of expressing it. Of the numerous definitions, there is the vital one that we've been discussing that illustrates the difference between choosing to live off one's healthy solution or one's unhealthy solution. As we've learned, it involves the notion of the perception we have of ourselves as individuals. This includes the realization that we have both positive and negative characteristics along with strengths and limitations.

Therefore, thinking in terms of all the dynamics involved in the notion of our two lifestyle solutions, healthy and unhealthy, it can be said that when we say we love someone, we should be saying two things. The first is that we love ourselves. The second is that we care so much for another person that we want to give our love to that person.

When one first hears this definition of love and the two components involved, it might at first sound rather egotistical. You love yourself so much you are willing to give yourself to another? However, we need to take a look at the opposite thought. If the "I love you" that is expressed to a partner does not have an element of self-love, then what are we actually giving to another when we make this statement of love? "I don't really like myself, but I hope you accept me anyway." How could this ever be considered love? What would we be giving if we did not love the qualities we have?

Eventually it becomes evident in therapy that most marital problems occur because there is a lack of self-love. The lack of self-love and self-respect creates inner unhappiness and discontent. When one or both partners live in this state of personal unhappiness, it automatically affects the way they relate to their partners. A partner who does not take pride in what he or she has to give a spouse offers very little. M. Scott Peck reminds us how important this concept is not only for ourselves, but also for the marriage itself. He explains, "Submission to love does not mean being a doormat. Just as throughout our lives we must choose what is and what is not our responsibility, so we must also choose, even if we are submitted to love, when to love others and when to love ourselves."[3]

Loving yourself does not mean you think you are a superior, extraordinary and wonderful human being. We have all met people who are conceited and overbearing and they are not about love. Rather, self-love means that you understand who you are. You see and accept your positives and negatives, strengths and limitations. You understand that you have fears and that you often feel vulnerable. You have feelings of inferiority. You accept these aspects of yourself and are trying to live your life with courage. By loving your entire self, there is no need to defend your limitations.

This acceptance frees you from the need to focus defensively on yourself. Since you accept vulnerability, you do not need to waste energy on building walls around your ego. When you feel inferior or experience anxiety, it does not come as a surprise. You know you have a choice of either spending your time trying to nullify the feeling or accepting it in a way that is not dictated by it and then moving on. You do not dislike yourself because you have limitations. By choosing the healthy solution, based on self-love, you are free to care for others and to love them genuinely.

With the recognition of our basic humanness, we can love who we are and we are free to use the gifts we have as loving human beings. We can choose not to be defensive about our shortcomings. We know love is not like looking in a mirror at ourselves and saying, "My, my, how wonderful." Rather, we are introspective and see the reflections of who we are and like the people we have become. We also like who we are becoming. The values and priorities we admire have become part of our natures. We have a belief system we try to follow in everything we do.

Then, in the most meaningful act we can perform, we so love other people that we want to share our personal gifts and the gifts of life with our partners. When our partners are doing the same—loving who they are and wanting to share that—the marital possibilities are endless. Both people see the love the other has to give. They see the other cherishes life and cherishes his or her gifts. They see what the other has become and recognize that person's desire to become even more. Love between two people is sharing the act of becoming!

Marriage is the ultimate challenge of love—the love of self and love for another. In no other area is full cooperation so necessary. In order to achieve this level of love, it is mandatory we know both our healthy and unhealthy solutions. It is also mandatory we take the time to know our partners' dual solutions. Adler emphasizes this point when he explains the importance of realizing, "Love by itself does not solve everything, and it is better to rely on work, interest and cooperation to solve the problems of the marriage."[4]

This begins by knowing each other's fears and vulnerabilities. Spouses hopefully spend hours talking to each other, sharing feelings and thoughts about themselves. As they face life's challenges and deal with problems, sharing fears and vulnerabilities needs to be a primary part of any conversation. It requires open and honest discussion. A love relationship starts with the willingness and desire to be fully open to our partners. It starts with the willingness and desire to know our partners.

A love relationship, therefore, involves being with another person with whom you can be vulnerable. We should not hide who we truly are from our spouses. Unsuccessful marriages always carry with them an element of dishonesty. Successful marriages have the building block where each person cares and loves the other so much that each is even concerned about the other's fears and vulnerabilities. These spouses encourage these inferiorities to be discussed openly and honestly. They want to help their partners to stay on healthy tracks. They want, above all, to be sensitive to their partners' humanness. They want to be partners in creating an open and honest life together.

Love Requires Honesty

Most of the conflicts and arguments in a marriage are the result of one or both partners refusing to be honest about who they are and what they are intrinsically experiencing as far as feeling inferior or vulnerable. Denial of the real self by either partner leads to hiding and defensiveness in the marriage. We have discussed how the denial of humanness leads one down a neurotic path and impinges on the creative self. The same is true when denial takes place in a marriage. In neurosis, the creative and loving self is overshadowed by the need to achieve the psychological ideal or the perfect image one wants of oneself. The true self is replaced by the need to counteract all negative feelings about self.

When either partner in a marriage chooses to hide his or her fears and vulnerabilities or tries to cover up any inferiorities or inadequacies, the partner puts him or herself in the position of acting defensively in most interactions. Rather than responding openly to who he or she truly is and being honest about his or her feelings regarding what is taking place in the marriage, the partner chooses to lie and pretend to be someone else.

Dishonesty creates confusion and distance between the partners.

The degree each person hides his or her true feelings when a conflict occurs equals the degree the problems are badly handled. The degree either person feels the need to be defensive is the degree resentment is eventually created between the partners. The degree either partner does not admit to his or her humanness equals the degree the relationship becomes a sham.

Partners in a healthy marriage realize it is normal to experience limitations. They realize fears and vulnerabilities will come to the surface when facing a challenge. They realize that perhaps more than any other situation in one's life, the marital relationship holds the most possibilities for these vulnerabilities to be tapped and exposed. There are so many challenges in every marriage. Realizing and being open to how each challenge affects our partners and ourselves becomes vital to having a healthy relationship. Deceiving oneself and one's partner about feelings of inferiority and vulnerability is at the core of all marital conflicts. It is when either partner refuses to be honest about how he or she feels regarding a particular situation that the trouble begins. Our defensive mechanisms are basically lies. Lies create walls where we lose sight not only of our true selves, but of the true selves of our partners as well.

Seeing Marriage as Becoming a Person

Let's remember all marital relationships are permeated with challenges. It is challenging, because we are human beings who are vulnerable and imperfect and are tested by so many areas of life. One goal of this book is for partners to learn how to see these challenges from another perspective. Each of the real life stories we've observed depicts couples experiencing problems and issues that can happen to any one of us.

In the marital cases I've presented, you witnessed couples who took on the marital challenge and those who did not. Hopefully, learning of these experiences, you have concluded that the real challenge of marriage is twofold. There is the challenge of finding or staying on your own healthy track and the added responsibility to help your partner to be as healthy and creative as possible. This challenge entails acting as a therapist for yourself and for your spouse, while allowing your partner to do the same for you.

The challenge takes patience, time and continuous effort. It is ongoing. The challenge calls for each person to admit when ordeals can be overwhelming. It requires each partner to recognize and admit to his or her own feelings of inferiority, vulnerability and fear as the challenges are being met. With an openness regarding human beings' basic nature, marriage requires that each partner acknowledge he or she can give in to these fears and react defensively. Each partner is challenged to diagnose his or her own neurotic track and to see how it is often used as a defensive response to specific personal vulnerabilities. By being fully open to this lifestyle track, the goal is to see that there are choices we make in response to our marital challenges. One choice denies fears and inferiorities, distracting one from responding to a problem. The other choice admits to these feelings of vulnerability but does not let it hinder creatively responding to the problem presented.

Time and effort is also required by each partner to figure out the other partner's fears and vulnerabilities and to what extent the partner operates with a solution that protects these feelings. Once this task is begun, it becomes the partner's responsibility to help the person he or she loves come to terms with these fears and to see that he or she has a choice other than one of defense and denial.

Performing these lifestyle assessments is the challenge of marriage. We must all remember that none of us really wants to change, for changing always exposes fears and inferiorities. We need not fear this reality nor consider it negative; if it is done knowing the positive consequences, it can bring confidence and joy to both.

We get tired and worn out by outside variables. We know how they can cause frustration and carry the temptation to just give in. Marriage, however, is the one place where two people can respond to these challenges and support each other. The key is to recognize these problems for what they are and to help each other respond to them openly and creatively. As problems arise, it is mandatory that blame and finger-pointing be avoided at all cost. When the goal of having a loving relationship overrides the need to protect oneself, then marriage becomes an environment that is full of possibilities.

Marriage is never a one-way street. It demands mutual cooperation. With openness and insight, we can see how, as couples, both negative and positive tracks interconnect us. It does little good to deny this reality or to hide from it. In fact, facing our inferiorities and fears is the only way to grow and to be truly ourselves. Marriage needs to be the place we can find freedom and openness about who we are. Marriage, more than any other part of life, is the most fertile area for personal growth. So much good can come from a relationship where the partners truly understand and accept the facts of their humanness. Marriage allows two people to practice the art of becoming people. The challenge is to know we have a choice. The challenge is to help each other, using love and respect, with the choices we make each step of the way. Accepting this challenge promises many wonderful and beautiful results.

Mending a Relationship

Couples enter marital counseling in varying degrees of conflict. It can range from a full openness by both partners to improve their marital situations to a great deal of rage, anger and finger-pointing. In many situations, the initial session follows a recent marital crisis. The initiation of therapy is often on the request of only one of the partners, meaning one partner might not be fully committed and ready to confront problems in the relationship. In order to encourage the full participation of both partners, a number of major points need to be addressed in order to lay the foundation for the healing of the relationship.

All marital problems must first be seen as individual problems. There is no such thing in a relationship where one partner is totally at fault. We all bring our unhealthy and sometimes damaging issues into the relationships with our spouses. The key, therefore, to creating a loving and working relationship and mending one that has gone astray is the recognition and admission by both partners of their human imperfections and how these imperfections may be affecting their relationship.

The first step is to become aware of how each individual, based on the very nature of his or her humanness, experiences feelings of inferiority and various levels of fear. Both partners also experience anxieties created by a wide range of physical, mental and emotional vulnerabilities. In the counseling process, sometimes individual sessions are required to identify these fears and vulnerabilities. This gives each partner the opportunity and freedom to focus on him or herself. Without the presence of the other partner, it allows the finger-pointing and underlying discontent toward the other partner to stop. It gives each partner the chance to identify personal issues, to own them for what they are and to start seeing marital issues from a wider perspective.

This wider perspective must entail the very important fact that we bring both healthy solutions and unhealthy solutions into the marital relationship. The unhealthy solution is a partner's attempt to avoid, as much as possible, all fears and vulnerabilities. In this sense, it has nothing to do with the relationship, for when either partner is using this unhealthy solution it is all about him or her. This level of awareness takes courage to admit, but it is mandatory for the true healing of the relationship.

Once both of the partners have identified their core fears and feelings of inferiority, they can return to counseling together with a better understanding of how they as individuals are affected by problems and challenges within the marriage. They are also able to address how they might fall into the trap of responding to these problems with their unhealthy and defensive solutions. Even if one partner is more fixated on his or her defensive solution, it helps each partner to see the other in a different light. Too often marital conflicts are taken personally and as attacks when in fact the partner is not actually attacking his or her spouse, but more protecting him or herself. Objective understanding of this fact lessens the sting and hurt compared to when it is taken as a personal affront.

It takes a great deal of courage to approach marital conflicts in this manner. It is much easier to spend each session pointing out the faults of a partner. Couples need to become aware of the destructiveness of this approach. It resolves nothing and usually leads to further separation.

Arguing back and forth, verbally jabbing and punching each other and continuing with the interactions that probably take place at home lead spouses into a useless cycle of more discontent and misdirected energy. Weekly sessions that act as punching matches must be replaced with honest communication and a desire to reconnect. It also allows the therapist to go from being a referee to a healer. Healing and learning to operate with a healthy solution is what it is all about.

Lori and Bill's Story

Lori and Bill had been married for fourteen years and had one child. They both admitted they had been growing apart, especially during the past five to seven years. The couple initiated therapy in the middle of a major conflict. It was not a new dispute, but one that had surfaced on many occasions over the previous five years. Both defined their issue in similar fashion but disagreed vehemently as to its cause.

Lori admitted that she was going out socially more frequently. She explained, "The more I go out, the more I realize how bored I am at home. I need some sort of fulfillment. I want to love Bill, but more often than not he's just not there."

In response, Bill explained:

I am angry and upset. What is going on is not normal for a marriage. She is always on the phone or e-mailing someone. I feel there is something else going on. It is not just friends to whom she talks. She talks to a lot of men. When I confront her she says she is sorry but then does it again.

Lori did not deny Bill's accusations. She had already mentioned she was going out a great deal and she also admitted to talking on the phone to a few men. In her defense she said:

There is nothing physical going on as Bill thinks. It could be an emotional affair, but it is nothing more. I keep telling Bill I need more from him. I know what I am doing looks wrong, but when I do it, I don't feel lonely or depressed. We were close at one time. I don't know what happened to that.

To get a better picture of the psychological lifestyles of Lori and Bill, they each attended a few individual counseling sessions. In sessions with Bill, his early recollections revealed a strong fear of being embarrassed and also a fear of being on his own. In one of his recollections he stated, "I was sitting in a speedboat with friends. I slipped off the boat without a life preserver and was under the boat. It was scary." He had a recurring dream as a child that was similar to his early recollection. He told me, "I was driving, but I could not see. I couldn't stop the car and was scared that I might hit something."

Understanding and accepting the philosophy regarding the nature of being human, Bill began to see some of the underlying fears he was carrying. After a number of insightful conversations with me, Bill began to put the pieces together. He was an only child whose father died when he was eight years old. His mother he described as very nice but obsessed with neatness and afraid to do things. She had a nervous breakdown when he was in college. Then Bill admitted, "I think I am a lot like her."

Even though Bill remained angry over Lori's behavior, he began to see that he also had issues. Putting his anger to rest for awhile, he started to see, from a lifestyle viewpoint, why he was attracted to Lori. With a great deal of honesty, he explained:

> I was attracted to Lori physically, but also because she had a great personality. She was very outgoing and, unlike me, had a lot of friends. On dates we went all over the place doing crazy things. I am more to myself and Lori did most of the initiating. I have a hard time coming up with something to say.

Based on his underlying fears and poor self-perspective, Bill found this information about himself difficult to acknowledge. Eventually he found the courage to see the purpose at the core of a lot of his behavior. With this acceptance of how fear was dictating his life, he began to see the changes he needed to make if he was ever going to live a fuller life and make his marriage healthier.

In Lori's first individual session she expressed her disappointment about the marriage. She explained, "I never imagined this happening. But, especially during the last five years, I am getting less and less out of my marriage." Just as Bill's early recollections revealed a great deal, so did Lori's. Her first two recollections revealed some of her intrinsic fears and needs and what might be dictating her behavior. She clearly stated:

> I was riding my new bike down the street and suddenly fell. I was almost hit by a car. I rode home and my parents were nonchalant. My parents were not emotionally available to me.

> A strange man came up to me when I was walking home from school. I ran home and banged on the door. At first it was locked. When my parents answered, I told them about what happened. They had no reaction.

Lori's recurring dream was also revealing and reinforced the insights presented in her early recollections. She explained, "I was someplace and realized I was lost. I looked around for whomever I was with and couldn't find the person. I felt alone." The second oldest of four children, Lori explained that her older sister got most of the attention. She described both her parents as dysfunctional. She explained, "My parents were alcoholics. They were very social but had little time for me and my siblings."

Lori was as open as Bill when it came time to putting the pieces of her lifestyle together. She saw that she had a tremendous fear of abandonment, along with a deep-seated hurt caused by rejection. To counteract her own personal terrors, she sought the attention of as many people as she could for reassurance and love.

Returning to therapy together, Lori and Bill were ready to share with each other what they had learned. They both admitted they were on their personally devised neurotic paths that were created to compensate for their fears and inferiority. Perhaps more importantly, especially in terms of their marital relationship, they were able to realize how their solutions were counterproductive to each other's needs.

Bill and Lori had a lot of work ahead of them if their marriage was to have a chance. Because of their honesty and willingness to self-reflect, they began to see themselves and each other in a much different light. Recognizing the destructiveness of their unhealthy solutions, they made a commitment to each other to change and to support the other in this process. As their weekly sessions proceeded, they began to bring out the best in each other. In doing so, they respected each other's vulnerabilities and needs. With this respect, they sought to fulfill each other in much more productive ways.

As a therapist I am often asked if people can really change. Underlying that question is "Does therapy really work?" My answer is always a definitive yes, but it depends on the capability and desire of each individual or couple in therapy. Bill and Lori had all the tools for making counseling a success. They were intelligent, they were open about themselves as individuals and they had the desire to fix a relationship that was slowly deteriorating.

Claire and Charlie's Story

Claire and Charlie are another couple who came to realize how change is possible and how much it depends on one's willingness to do the work. They explained they were married late in life by society's standards, both being forty years old at the time. Claire explained, "We both wanted children right away, especially due to our ages. With the help of medicine, we ended up with triplets. It was a shock at first, but we wanted children so much. The children are now five years old."

Charlie followed by saying, "The children are part of the issue but not all of it. To be honest, I recently told Claire that I was not happy. I don't feel we have a relationship like we once did."

Claire said she did not realize that Charlie was so unhappy and explained, "I want to address this now before it gets worse. I have so many friends who are divorced or unhappy. We need help." Charlie also admitted that the problem he was having was not just with Claire but with all the stress in their lives. He explained:

We had to put an addition on the house right away for the children. Financially it put us in a hole. On top of it, Claire is a collector. The house is full of stuff. She spends so much time with things we don't even need. She wants me to help with things I have no interest in.

To get a sense of the underlying factors that might be dictating each of their lives, I reviewed both Claire's and Charlie's early recollections and recurring dreams. Then I took into consideration their birth order positions and how they might have affected Claire's and Charlie's perceptions of life. We also discussed their family histories and their relationships with their parents and siblings. In this counseling situation, both Claire and Charlie chose to go through the process in couple's sessions.

Charlie was the oldest of five children. With full realization, he took on the role of being the oldest very seriously. However, with the typical responsibilities of the oldest child, he experienced a number of setbacks. His first recollection encompassed the feelings he acquired as a result of this difficult big brother role. Charlie shared:

I was about four years old. We had just moved to a new house. My younger brother and I were running around the house and he fell. He had to get stitches. My mother was upset and I felt bad. I felt guilty, like it was my fault since he was chasing me.

There were a number of instances in Charlie's childhood where he felt guilt or embarrassment about how situations turned out. He expressed that he could see how his role was overwhelming and that it was probably unfair that he saw all these things as his responsibilities. What Charlie did not realize was that he was carrying the same approach into his adult life and his marriage. The triplets were one thing, the overwhelming finances were another and finally, he was feeling less than worthy due to the lack of attention from Claire. He repeated, "She is always busy with stuff."

Claire was an attentive listener and she began to see her husband in a different light. She was also able to learn a great deal from her own lifestyle examination. Even though they were both able to identify the outside pressures that were draining them, they needed to become aware of how they were being tapped by these challenges and what solutions they were bringing to them. Two of Claire's early recollections revealed not only her fears, but also her possible solution and approach to problems. She revealed:

> We had just moved to Maryland. I was standing in the kitchen and holding on to my father's leg. I felt happy and content.

> My sister and I were fighting. My father came up and started hitting my sister. I pulled the sheet over my head until he got tired and stopped. I was shocked he got to this point.

After explaining what to look for in early recollections—what the fear is and the solution to the fear—Claire could easily see a dependency in the first recollection and a solution of hiding when problems occur in the second. After gaining a great deal of information regarding each of their psychological approaches to life's challenges, I asked Claire and Charlie to see their issues in the marriage from this vantage point.

Charlie was taking on too much in the big brother role and feeling responsible when things did not work out. At the same time, with Claire's lack of attention, he was not getting any satisfaction from what he was trying to do. The challenges and Claire's lack of feedback all were interpreted as failure. The end result was more and more instances of unhappiness for Charlie.

Looking over her childhood experiences and the conclusions she reached from them, Claire was able to see a certain dependency on others for her contentment. She also could see that she often hid from challenges—pulled the sheet over her head—and turned her attention to things she could control (the stuff in the house). In doing so, she was not showing any appreciation for all the things Charlie was doing.

Because Charlie and Claire were so open to learning about themselves, we had a great deal to work with at the counseling sessions.

Openness like this can lead to rewarding results. Charlie and Claire, along with Bill and Lori, were able to turn their marriages around simply because they were willing to do the work necessary to accomplish this change. With the foundation of love, it takes honesty, reflection and forgiveness. It takes learning how to love yourself for the gifts you have and then respecting the gifts of your spouse. It takes learning from the past, so the future will be brighter and filled with hope.

Part Five

Making Marriage Last

In this book my goal was to take the mystery out of why some marriages fail while others succeed and help couples make their unions more fulfilling forever. I also wanted to reveal why some long-term marriages seem to end so abruptly and supposedly without warning. I strongly believe, based on many years of counseling conflicted partners, that living years within a marriage without cherishing our human gifts removes our ability to love ourselves and to love others. The obsession with self-image in terms of our limitations and faults blinds us from envisioning the power of love. A partner who is fixated on perfecting his or her self-image destroys not only his or her potential, but also the potential for a love relationship.

Too many people start out their marriages in states of forgetfulness, avoidance and denial. As the years of marriage go on, one or both partners intensify this mind-set with a need to void all limitations. I firmly feel that the act of focusing on limitations becomes a limitation in and of itself. In marriages that are destructive for years and years, spouses painfully forget they were created to love and be loved in the first place. In marriages where each partner respects him or herself as part of creation, the love relationship has no boundaries.

The case histories presented throughout this book illustrate how some couples are able to make their relationships nourishing and productive and others do not. In my experience as a counselor and my research, I have found that the couples who succeed accept the human condition of being imperfect. They have the courage to face the reality that inferiority, anxiety and fear are part of their lives. Yet, they do not allow these potential obstacles to interfere with their creativity and relationship. These are the reasons they are able to be successfully intimate—mentally, emotionally and physically.

An important component is that partners in successful relationships must be honest, both individually and with the other partner. They need to and do accept the starting premise that no human has what it takes to handle all the challenges and problems of life. They acknowledge there will be times when they or their partners will focus too much on their vulnerabilities and allow these thoughts and feelings to dictate their moods and behaviors. This admission about themselves and their partners allows an all-encompassing honesty and openness toward each other. It allows both partners to see they have a choice of whether to be healthy or not. Finally, it allows partners to help their spouses in making this choice.

The goal of individual therapy is to have each person identify their personal feelings of inferiority and their vulnerable buttons that cause anxiety and fear. They know that, as imperfect human beings, there will be times when they will fall into their unhealthy and neurotic tracks. Their task is to know this track thoroughly and be open to the times when they make such mistakes. The challenge then is to return to a healthy and creative approach to the problems they are facing. In this sense, marital therapy is the same as individual therapy, but the former is twofold.

Marital counseling involves the same awareness but is focused on the relationship of two people. One definition of a healthy person is when the person knows his or her fears and unhealthy solutions and chooses not to live in that manner. Similarly, in a healthy marriage both partners know they have fears and anxieties and they know the other partner also has his or her points of vulnerability. Each partner is aware he or she can be unhealthy at times, as is true of his or her partner. The awesome opportunity in a love relationship is the willingness of both partners to help each other be healthy and creative as much as possible.

Pam and Doug's Story

Pam and Doug came to marriage counseling six months after Doug was involved in a major car accident. The accident was serious and all agreed Doug was lucky to be alive. Initially, however, Doug had to deal with a number of cognitive issues due to the major concussion he experienced as a result of the accident. Over time many of these issues improved, but he still struggled with some speech problems and some areas of memory retention. Two months after the accident he also experienced a seizure.

I perceived in the counseling sessions that Pam and Doug, married for twenty-eight years, loved each other very much. However, due to the fact that their vulnerabilities were exposed and a range of fears were overwhelming their thoughts, they were starting to get on each other's nerves. Doug, who suffered a brain injury in the accident, was having a hard time accepting his newly acquired physical and mental limitations. In reality, they acted as obstacles in everyday interactions with his wife and children and affected his returning to work. There were days when he was consumed with a deep depression and could not eat or sleep.

Pam was filled with worry regarding the welfare of her husband. Even though Doug received full clearance following his seizure, Pam was overly careful in what she allowed him to do. As her anxieties increased, her list of don'ts also became longer. In many of her conversations with Doug, she voiced fears and worries which became a constant reminder to him of his new limitations, many of them now exaggerated by Pam. In like manner, many of Doug's attempts to return to some level of normalcy tapped into Pam's worries and fears about Doug's well-being and the thought of another accident or seizure. In each of their attempts to lessen their personal fears and anxieties, they were becoming annoying and hurtful to each other.

From the outset, both Doug and Pam were enthusiastic about the prospects and insights counseling could offer them. They both were confident in their love for each other but could see that their personal fears were overtaking the positives in their relationship. Doug was depressed by his medical condition but was working hard on what he could do rather than focusing on his newly acquired limitations. There were times when he fell into despair and had thoughts that all his efforts were a waste of time. Pam's list of things Doug should not do was rigidly adhered to at times. She could not see how she was filling Doug with anger and an increased sense of hopelessness.

Counseling offered Doug and Pam the opportunity to verbalize their fears and worries. In one of the sessions Pam clearly stated, "I am so afraid of something else happening to Doug. I am so afraid of losing him." Each day of interaction with each other became permeated with their fears and worries. Even though Pam's feelings were certainly normal and expected, she needed to recognize that her fears were dictating her relationship with Doug, who was trying to move forward as best he could after his accident.

During one session I said to Pam, "Pam, you have to get the coffin out of the house." At first, Pam was taken aback by such a harsh statement. Because of her ability to pause and reflect, Pam soon recognized how there were times she was being more destructive than helpful to Doug's recovery. At the same time, Doug identified how his times of despair and depression, as normal as they were, were also reinforcing Pam's worries and vulnerabilities.

As a result of productive counseling sessions, Doug and Pam's willingness to be open to the notions of human vulnerability and to the possibility of having unhealthy solutions increased. They acquired a new perspective about themselves and each other. As time went on they were able to respect each other's feelings and help each other not to fall into unhealthy defensive behavior. They recognized that many of their responses to this crisis were attempts to control the future and therefore control their levels of vulnerability. With a new awareness, they reached a point where they could support each other and return to a healthier solution. Knowing they still had work to do, they became partners in helping each other stay on their healthy tracks while dealing with a very difficult situation.

Keys to a Successful Marriage

Both individual and marital therapy take a great deal of hard work and courage. Initially, no one revels in the fact that he or she might have flaws or that his or her behavior might be inappropriate. However, a person must be able to see and acknowledge that by avoiding these revelations, it does not mean they will go away. For any marriage to be truly success-ful, each partner must face the fact that within his or her makeup there is a powerful need to avoid all feelings of inferiority and vulnerability. Throughout a marriage it can be expected that the fulfillment of these needs will become part of the marital relationship. In too many cases, they unfortunately become a primary part of the relationship.

This recognition is the key to a successful relationship. The full acknowledgment of our human condition allows for creativity and nourishment. This is the beauty of being a human being. If we were perfect in every way, there would be no choice. We are not forced to love ourselves or to love others. We have the freedom to make our own choices. Forced love is not real. Only when there are alternatives can the options we choose have any validity. The challenge of being human is how we go about making these choices.

Marriages are filled with challenges. The vows we all take as we make a commitment to another person define the mission and under-taking that is before us. In good times and bad times, we promise to stick together. On our wedding days these challenges have not yet been given a name, but the wise know it is part of the journey: finances, rais-ing children, sickness (both physical and mental), sexual temptations, competition and the response to events we have little or no control over are just some of the areas that constantly require our attention. We need to be aware that these will ignite our human fears and uncover the vulnerabilities of being human. If we accept this condition for what it is and allow ourselves to focus on our abilities and not our limitations, we are in a position to generate a movement towards success.

Fostering and nourishing a relationship requires the growth and continuous expansion of each partner. There are marriages that last a long time, but unless there is the excitement for the new and the craving for development, these marriages soon become passive states of misery and suffering. For many partners, the passivity of personal unhappiness turns into acts of draining and, at times, destructive behavior towards each other. There is only one way to avoid this fateful outcome. It is in response to our inner hunger for self-acceptance and self-love and the desire to share our gifts with another. With each partner working from this platform, couples will journey together on a voyage of love and creativity.

Self-respect and respect for our partners act as roots for successful growth. From there, each partner must decide on how and where he or she wants to grow. Through trial and error, each must assess individual strengths and interests. Some of these may be similar to a partner's wishes, but many will be the individual yearnings of just one partner. The sharing of these personal gifts and the goals that are achieved through them become the life blood of a heart-filled relationship. Honoring one's own gifts and achievements and paying tribute to the gifts and achievements of one's partner promises a relationship that is constantly revitalized and energized.

As a therapist, I have witnessed cases where one partner has achieved success and the spouse has yet to recognize it. The first partner receives acclaim from others but not from the primary person in his or her life. The second partner has lost the opportunity to praise and honor his or her spouse. Perhaps more than a lost moment, it becomes an insult. Omission is many times more damaging than an actual act.

There are couples who watch a classic and deeply-felt movie at a local theater, yet silently return to the car without a moment of sharing. One or both partners were certainly touched by the theme and storyline. One or both is filled with a sense of life's possibilities and the realness of life's pendulum, from deep sadness to the heights of joy. Yet the partners decide to keep such soulful experiences to themselves. Is it because the other partner, based on repetitive past experiences, is presumed to lack understanding? Or have they already fallen into a rut that automatically omits conversation of this type? In either case, another chance for sharing is regrettably missed.

Other counseling sessions have revealed situations where one or both partners cannot forgive. One partner's behavior, either a singular event or an ongoing pattern, has created wounds that have yet to heal. The harmful actions of one partner have offended the other partner's self-worth and that person has a hard time getting it back. In these times of marital crisis, each partner must try to become more objective.

The offending partner must be able to explain to the other mate how and why he or she fell into an unhealthy solution. The offended partner must then reach a level of understanding that moves away from taking it all personally. Certainly this takes a great deal of strength. Yet, the fact is that when either partner acts in an unhealthy manner, the reasons for such behavior are all about him or her, not about the spouse. Openness to the reality of mistakes followed by a genuine forgiveness allows both partners to return to their connection on their healthy tracks.

Mutual Support

Successful partners in marriages share dreams and goals. Partners celebrate accomplishments and they rush to share with each other when they have been touched by a book, a movie or a conversation with someone. They want to make their relationship interesting and alive. So many relationships start out this way, but then one or the other or both soon forget the seeds that gave birth to the love between them.

When some of these marriages end in the divorce courts, each partner may think he or she knows the reasons. One or both partners, however, often miss the point. The tendency is to emphasize the consequences of their lifestyles but not the personal lifestyles themselves. If the spouses knew better, if they understood the psychology of human beings and the psychology of love relationships, the chances would have increased that their marital journey would have taken a much different route and had a much different ending.

This becomes the goal of marital counseling: reviving the multiple ways spouses were originally connected, assessing the many missed opportunities and encouraging them to seek within themselves and their partners a rebirth to love's possibilities. It is basic common sense, yet is so often lost in the entanglements of life's chores and outside challenges. Even so, the basic truth lies before all who are responding to the challenges of marriage. The more people experience self-fulfillment and receive fulfillment from their partners, the more their relationships continue to grow and remain a satisfying and dynamic connection.

Continuing the Journey

On the day one of my daughters was married, as her father I had the privilege to give the wedding toast at the reception. I reminded both my daughter and her husband of the gifts each of them was bringing into the marriage. I told them that these gifts must be nourished and protected. Like other couples, my daughter and her husband will be challenged during their years of marriage by many outside influences and forces. When they have children, as much as they will bring enormous joy and happiness, they will also tap into an immense vulnerability in each of them. As every parent will concur, there will be worries each time the children step out the door.

I explained to my daughter and son-in-law that they will also be challenged by the values and morals of society. In so many circumstances they will find an environment that is filled with competition, the striving for individual power and an individual's selfish concerns that have nothing to do with the welfare of others. There will be the challenge of finances and the cost of raising a family. Being a husband and wife, being parents and keeping their careers together will awake anxieties and vulnerabilities in each of them.

As much as all of these challenges call on spouses' creativity and can potentially bring out the best in them, they will also create moments of self-doubt and worry about each of their abilities to respond to all that is before them. It is at these moments when spouses must come together as a couple and remind each other of the gifts each of them has within. For their marriage to stay healthy, they need to renew the feelings that brought them to their wedding day throughout their marriage.

All problematic marriages are individual problems first. It starts when either partner ceases to see him or herself as lovable or to see his or her partner as lovable as well. It occurs when a person wants to rid him or herself of all human anxiety and demands perfection from him or herself in everything. Love takes work and patience. With love, however, the marital relationship will always remain creative and will always bring with it the promise of new horizons.

I would like to present a similar toast to the one I gave my daughter and her husband at their wedding reception to all of you. You have taken the time to explore this book with me. This means you value yourself and you value the relationship between you and your partner. You care enough to nourish yourself with ideas and further understanding. You value your mate and want to give him or her the lovable and loving you. For this I toast and praise you and wish you all the best in your and your partner's satisfying, fulfilling relationship: your journey through life together.

Notes

Preface

1 Stephanie Chen, "Why call it quits after decades of marriage?" CNN Living, June 2, 2010, http://articles.cnn.com/2010-06-02/living/al.gore.separation.40years.marriage_1_divorce-marriage-experts-couples?_s=PM:LIVING.

2 Anita Creamer, "Baby boomers lead new wave of 'gray divorce'", *The Sacramento Bee,* August 15, 2010, http://www.sacbee.com/2010/08/15/2959874/baby-boomers-lead-new-wave-of.html?storylink=lingospot.

3 Chen, "Why call it quits after decades of marriage?"

4 Thomas Moore, *Soul Mates* (New York: Harper Collins, 1994), xiv.

Part One

1 Moore, *Soul Mates,* xviii.

2 M. Scott Peck, *The Road Less Traveled and Beyond* (New York: Simon & Schuster, 1997), 25.

3 Ibid., 23.

4 Alfred Adler, *Superiority and Social Interest* (New York: W.W. Norton & Co., 1979), 220.

5 Rowena Ansbacher and Heinz Ansbacher, eds., *The Individual Psychology of Alfred Adler* (New York: Harper and Row, 1956), 254.

6 Peck, *The Road Less Traveled and Beyond,* 54.

7 R. Ansbacher and H. Ansbacher, *The Individual Psychology of Alfred Adler,* 350.

8 Ibid., 351.

9 Ibid., 351.

10 Ibid., 358.

11 Karen Horney, *Neurosis and Human Growth* (New York: W.W. Norton, 1950), 349.

12 R. Ansbacher and H. Ansbacher, *The Individual Psychology of Alfred Adler,* 377.

13 Ibid., 378.

14 Ibid., 379.

15 Ibid., 380.

16 Ibid., 380.

17 Ibid., 296.

18 Horney, *Neurosis and Human Growth,* 203.

19 Ibid., 215.

[20] Ibid., 220.
[21] Ibid., 221.
[22] R. Ansbacher and H. Ansbacher, *The Individual Psychology of Alfred Adler*, 432.
[23] Peck, *The Road Less Traveled and Beyond*, 27.

Part Two
[1] Stephen Covey, *The Seven Habits of Highly Effective Families* (New York: Golden Books, 1997), 81.
[2] R. Ansbacher and H. Ansbacher, *The Individual Psychology of Alfred Adler*, 437.
[3] Moore, *Soul Mates*, 8.
[4] Ibid., 55.

Part Three
[1] Horney, *Neurosis and Human Growth*, 23-24.
[2] Elizabeth Kubler-Ross, *On Death and Dying* (New York: Scribner, 1969).
[3] Peck, *The Road Less Traveled and Beyond*, 122.
[4] R. Ansbacher and H. Ansbacher, *The Individual Psychology of Alfred Adler*, 254.
[5] Horney, *Neurosis and Human Growth*, 194.
[6] Ibid., 213.
[7] Ibid., 212.
[8] Ibid., 195.
[9] Peck, *The Road Less Traveled and Beyond*, 139.
[10] Horney, *Neurosis and Human Growth*, 200.
[11] Ibid., 220.
[12] Peck, *The Road Less Traveled* (New York: Touchstone Press, 1985), 144.
[13] Kubler-Ross, *On Death and Dying*, 124.
[14] William Paul Young, *The Shack* (California: Windblown Media, 2007).
[15] Moore, *Soul Mates*, 191-192.
[16] Horney, *Neurosis and Human Growth*, 357.
[17] Ernest Becker, *The Denial of Death* (New York: Macmillan Publishing Co., 1975), 261.
[18] Horney, *Neurosis and Human Growth*, 293.

Part Four
[1] R. Ansbacher and H. Ansbacher, *The Individual Psychology of Alfred Adler*, 437.
[2] Ibid., 434.
[3] Peck, *The Road Less Traveled and Beyond*, 149.
[4] R. Ansbacher and H. Ansbacher, *The Individual Psychology of Alfred Adler*, 434.

Acknowledgments

I especially want to thank my sister, Dr. Margaret Mahoney. Peg spent countless hours editing and making suggestions for clarity. I want to especially thank her for her encouragement and support.

I want to thank Dr. Joan S. Dunphy, publisher at New Horizon Press, for giving me the opportunity to enter the world of publishing. I also want to thank Joanna Pelizzoni for all the editing she did and her helpful suggestions for completing this book.

I would also like to thank all my clients. I realize that I have been truly blessed to have a career that allows for such closeness and honesty with other human beings. Each of my clients has taught me a great deal in our many conversations and given me the opportunity to grow with them.